André Ashby is a humble follower of Jesus and a seeker of His presence. His life is devoted to loving, worshipping, and walking with the Creator of the universe. He is a living example of someone set afire for the Lord. In this wonderful book, *Wild and Mighty Fire*, André invites you to step out of the status quo and enter into the glory of God. I highly recommend this book to all who are hungry and thirsty to experience a deeper relationship with Holy Spirit!

—*Dr. Ché Ahn*
Apostle, Harvest Apostolic Center
Founding pastor, HRock Church, Pasadena, CA
President, Harvest International Ministry

Friends of André Ashby have been trying to get him to write about his history with God for years, and you're about to find out why. For many years, I've admired André's honest wrestling with God, and the profound ways God has demonstrated His love through André, and to him as well. This book will challenge and provoke you to greater intimacy with God, and co-laboring with Him to see His glory revealed in the earth.

—*William Ford III*
Director, Marketplace Leadership
Christ for the Nations Institute
Author, *Created for Influence: Transforming Culture From Where You Are*

As I read this book by my friend, prophet André Ashby, two things were evident, both of which were ingredients for success during the birth of the church in Acts 4:33: God's great power and God's great grace. André draws our attention to both topics through his passion for the church to grow in first the knowledge, second the reception, and last the dispensing of these non-negotiable attributes. It was through these vehicles that the church gave effective witness to the resurrection of our Lord. This is something this book helps us to relearn.

—*Glenn Dunlop*
Senior leader, Karmel City Church, Belfast, Northern Ireland

André Ashby is uniquely qualified to write this book! He is a friend of the Holy Spirit and a carrier of God's glory. Andre writes with firsthand knowledge of the way of the Holy Spirit. You will laugh and maybe cry as you read this enlightening book. Enjoy it, drink it in, and then pray that powerful prayer over yourself and your family: "Come, Holy Spirit!" Watch what will happen to you after reading this book. Then make sure you share it with a friend!

—*Brian Simmons*
Lead translator, The Passion Translation Project

André Ashby's book, *Wild and Mighty Fire*, will whet your appetite to move in the power of the Holy Spirit, make you hungry for radical encounters that take you deeper into the heart of Jesus, and challenge you to a lifestyle of doing the greater works promised us through the Holy Spirit! If these are the longings of your heart, then this is a book you must read!

I had the privilege of serving and walking alongside Jill Austin for almost seventeen years. For a few years, André traveled with us to many cities and nations. I was struck by his humility, his extraordinary vocal gifting, the passionate prophetic songs the Lord gave him that would break open a room and change lives, his teaching and preaching gifts, the fiery anointing on his life, and his friendship with the Holy Spirit.

We need the Word of God and the Spirit of God to powerfully impact this world! André's book couples biblical truths with his radical adventures with the Holy Spirit, which can ignite your heart and set you on fire so you can also blaze a trail in God for others to follow!

—*Linda Valen*
Ministry director, Master Potter Ministries

André Ashby's book, *Wild and Mighty Fire*, contains simple but powerful revelation and wisdom from God that the body of Christ will appreciate. In a day when there is so much confusion and hype, André Ashby brings clarity and simplicity to how we are to follow the Lord. It is great to see a book come along that stirs up hunger for more of Holy Spirit. I truly believe this book will strengthen the faith and create a greater desire for Holy Spirit. Andre's insight that comes from his personal encounters with the Lord will definitely bless the reader.

—*Ryan C. Lee*
Lead pastor, Blessed International Revival Center, Anaheim, CA

I have known André since 1993 and have never met anyone like him. His story comes from a passion for Jesus that is both sovereign but transferable, as I have seen in so many meetings in which he has taught, ministered, and sung. His relationship with our dear friend, the prophet and spiritual mother Jill Austin, impacted him in a way that marked his own journey, which will now mark yours. André has one of the most unique operations of the manifest presence of God on the planet. His book tells stories that will provoke you to ask God for a lifestyle of friendship with the Holy Spirit. I was so excited to relive some of these experiences and also hear new stories.

Even more, I was so glad that André teaches out of these experiences some really fresh revelation so that we can have this anointing and friendship with the Holy Spirit that he does. In a time when the body of Christ needs a great awakening, a new "Jesus people" movement, André is releasing a book with one of the most important keys: visitation of the Holy Spirit.

—*Shawn Bolz*
Senior pastor, Expression58
Author, *Keys to Heavens Economy* and *Translating God*

We have been privileged to know André Ashby over the past twenty years and consider him part of our family. We can honestly say that because of the level of intimacy that André walks in with God, he carries His presence wherever he goes. Although his life has been filled with struggles, he has experienced God's faithfulness over and over again, and has chosen to be an overcomer.

André is accustomed to the presence of the Lord, and while he has shared some extraordinary stories with us in this book, these experiences only leave him longing for more. We highly recommend *Wild and Mighty Fire*, and believe that it will not only encourage you, but challenge you in your walk with Jesus. We hope that reading this book will inspire you to press in to know God in a deeper way and experience the power of His presence!

—*Craig and Suzy Nelson*
Founders, Miracles in the Marketplace International and the
School of Miracles & Ministry

WILD&
MIGHTY
FIRE

WILD & MIGHTY FIRE

Encounter the Power of the Holy Spirit

ANDRÉ ASHBY

WHITAKER
HOUSE

WILD AND MIGHTY FIRE:
Encounter the Power of the Holy Spirit

André T. Ashby
andash9@aol.com

ISBN: 978-1-64123-092-6
eBook ISBN: 978-1-64123-093-3
Printed in the United States of America
© 2019 by André Ashby

Whitaker House
1030 Hunt Valley Circle
New Kensington, PA 15068
www.whitakerhouse.com

Library of Congress Cataloging-in-Publication Data
Names: Ashby, André, author.
Title: Wild and mighty fire : encounter the power of the Holy Spirit / André
T. Ashby.
Description: New Kensington, PA : Whitaker House, 2019. |
Identifiers: LCCN 2018029697 (print) | LCCN 2018041608 (ebook) | ISBN
9781641230933 (e-book) | ISBN 9781641230926 (alk. paper)
Subjects: LCSH: Holy Spirit. | Ashby, André.
Classification: LCC BT121.3 (ebook) | LCC BT121.3 .A84 2019 (print) | DDC
277.3/083092 [B] --dc23
LC record available at https://lccn.loc.gov/2018029697

This book has been printed digitally and produced in a standard specification in order to ensure its continuing availability.

DEDICATION

While many leaders have taught me how to walk and minister with the Holy Spirit, two who have poured most profoundly into the foundation of my ministry are James Goll and Jill Austin. The first class I took at Grace Training Center was James Goll's. He was the one who called me out to minister through prophetic song. Jill Austin, my spiritual mother, followed the cloud and the fire of the Spirit like no one else I have known. Her entire life was about getting out of the way and simply inviting the Holy Spirit to come and do what He does. Her heart's cry, and mine, is that an entire generation of believers would sign up for the same adventure.

CONTENTS

FOREWORD

For over forty years, as I have traveled the globe in full-time vocational ministry, I have observed, partaken of, and eventually been a leader in various movements of the Holy Spirit. Each wave of Holy Spirit carries a distinct quality or characteristic of God the Father, but is always centered on the Son of God, Jesus Christ. It is an honor to be an ambassador for Christ whether before a small group of three people or a large gathering of over one hundred thousand people. What a great privilege it is to represent the Creator of the universe. But as no two snowflakes are identical, so also are the movements and messengers God raises up.

At times, having been in so many meetings for so many years, things start to become a bit of a blur for me, with all the details fading in the background. On the other hand, there are those divine moments that are etched in my mind that I carry as treasures close to my heart. My first encounter with André Ashby fits into this latter category.

I was ministering at one of the six congregational locations within the Kansas City Fellowship on a Sunday morning, completing a three-week series on "Varieties of Prophetic Anointings." I really did not know the members of this particular location, so I called out a young black man and invited him to do what I did. I spoke in tongues and then interpreted the gift into English. I told him to do the same. After that, I said we were going to sing in the Spirit and then sing the interpretation in English. I sang forth in the Spirit in my full baritone voice and then this humble gentleman opened wide his mouth and out came this angelic prophetic sound that pierced the atmosphere. So André and I met by prophetically singing together.

Well, that started our relationship, which continues twenty-five years later! Funny thing, he was a visitor that day. But he is not a visitor any more to the things of Holy Spirit. André is one of the premier prophetic singers in the land. He carries a mantle of fire that is the most similar to Jill Austin's than anyone on the planet. Now I can say that because it's the truth and I know. I was there as a part of this gentle giant's beginning and I will continue cheering him on into the new things that God has for him—like composing this book you now hold in your hand.

It is my great honor and delight to commend to you both the consecrated life of this gentle, fiery giant in Christ Jesus and the prophetic grace that rests upon him. Well done, André! Well done!

—*Dr. James W. Goll*
International best-selling author
Founder, Encounters Network Prayer Storm | GET eSchool

INTRODUCTION

Over three years ago, the Lord began speaking to me about the message of this book. "I'm looking for a church that will be led by My Spirit," He told me, "just as Israel was led through the wilderness by the pillar of cloud by day and the pillar of fire by night."

The people of Israel camped around the presence of God. When the presence moved, they moved. God had complete access to rearrange their lives in order to get them where He wanted them to go.

Romans 8:14 declares, *"For as many as are led by the Spirit of God, these are sons of God."* The proof we have given the Holy Spirit His rightful place in our lives is that when He shows up and begins to move—we follow. We trust Him to rearrange our lives.

The Spirit has one primary agenda: to lead us into the fullness of living as beloved sons and daughters who look and act like Jesus. Many believers have a hard time grasping the idea that Jesus's intimacy with the Father, His purity, passion, and character, and His works of power, authority, and compassion are not an unattainable ideal, but are the very Christian life available to us through the Holy Spirit. This is why we must give the Holy Spirit full access to all that we are.

In the pages ahead, I offer what I have learned about how to move with the Holy Spirit when He comes. I've seen Him come in so many ways over the past twenty years in ministry, and yet I know there is so much more to see in the years ahead. May we be the generation who invites Him to lead us into realms of intimacy and transformation that will meet the cry of His heart and ours. May we make a place for Him to move.

Come, Holy Spirit.

1

THE FIRE LADY

In 1992, while studying at the University of Missouri–Kansas City (UMKC) Conservatory of Music, I began attending a prayer meeting focused on Israel at Metro Christian Fellowship, the church where the International House of Prayer was born. One Friday night in December, I came to the meeting and was surprised to learn that we had a guest ministering to us that night, a woman I had never heard of before.

Instead of launching into a message, this woman merely said three words.

"Come, Holy Spirit."

It was as if a firebomb exploded in the room. People began to have encounters with the God of heaven that astounded me. There was no question in my mind that God was real and He was there in our midst. Angels began to move in the room as the Holy Spirit gripped people and released their destinies.

The woman didn't really touch or lay hands on anybody. God Himself was encountering His people. I immediately recognized that the relationship she had with the third person of the Godhead, the Holy Spirit, was very rare, but I also knew in my heart that I was created to do what she was doing. I knew I was called to move in the supernatural realms of the Holy Spirit, where all things are possible.

That woman was Jill Austin, and she became my spiritual mother. Everything I have learned about how to cooperate with the Holy Spirit and move with His power stems from my time ministering with Jill. Thus, the best way I know to introduce you to the Holy Spirit is to tell you about the woman who immersed me in Him.

THE POTTER HEARS GOD

Jill Austin came to the Lord during the height of the Jesus People movement, which swept the country in the late sixties and early seventies. In that movement, God visited the youth of the United States with life-altering revival. Many of our church leaders today came into the body of Christ during that time. It is my prayer that God will do it again. Father God, release another Jesus People movement, for Your holy name's sake!

Jill's first career was as an award-winning professional potter. As a recognized fine artist, she was invited to participate in a Christian art festival. Thousands of people attended, but all of the "messy" artists, like the potters, were set up on the lower field away from the main action and seemed to attract less attention. Jill began to create. When she looked up from the wheel, she saw that her meager audience had all left. She began to cry and prayed, "Lord, if this has no life in it, I don't want to do it anymore." As far as she was concerned, she was done making pottery at the festival.

Then a couple of kids came along and kept bugging her to make a pot. She finally relented and told them she would do it on the last day. The last day rolled around and the kids hadn't forgotten. Reluctantly, she agreed to make the pot.

As she centered the clay on the wheel, Jill heard the voice of the Lord. He began to say things like, "Before you were formed in your mother's womb, I knew you. I have a plan for your life. I will strengthen you. I will build you up."

She said to the Lord, "Wow, that's good."

"Well, if it's so good, why don't you repeat it?" He said.

So that's what she did. Then, when she finished making the vessel, she looked up. A crowd had gathered, and many were weeping. She knew then God had given her a gift, but she didn't know it was called prophecy. All she knew was that God had spoken and she had repeated His words.

NO SCRIPT—"JUST FOLLOW ME"

With the explosion of the Jesus People movement, the church Jill attended went from a couple of hundred to over a thousand in a very short period of time. They started bringing in bands on Saturday nights, and were looking for opening acts. The pastor called Jill into his office and said, "I hear you are doing stories on the potter's wheel."

"I've done one," she said.

"Well, I want you to do one this Saturday before the band performs."

Jill agreed. On Saturday, she showed up at church in her overalls, while the band was decked out in shiny black jackets. She later told me they looked at her like, "Where did you come from?"

When she walked over to the pastor, he asked, "Are you ready?"

"Yes, pastor, I'm ready."

"Do you have your script?"

"Script? What's a script?"

"The words you wrote down and memorized," he said. "The words you speak while you are making the pot."

She said, "Well, God speaks to me and I just repeat it."

The pastor shook his head. "No, you can't do it that way."

Suddenly stripped of confidence, she exclaimed, "You're right! I can't do it that way!"

Jill ran out of the office, found a broom closet, and put her face up against the mops. "Lord, I didn't know I needed a script, but I guess I do," she prayed. "I need a script." But no matter how hard she tried, nothing would come out—she later described it as a kind of spiritual constipation.

After a bit, she heard the pastor asking, "Where did she go?"

One of the band members said, "I think she's down the hall in the closet."

She heard them approach the closet door, and then they knocked.

"Yes, come in," she replied.

"No, you come out."

Nervously, Jill came out. The pastor and band member pushed her toward the stage, where she saw her wheel standing ready on the other side. She stepped up on stage and froze. Everything began to fade in and out. She said, "Oh no, Lord! I'm about to pass out!"

The Lord spoke to her. "You know Me, right?"

"Yes, Lord. I know You."

"And you know you're clay, right?"

"Yes, Lord."

"Just follow Me."

So she followed the Lord across the stage and sat down at the wheel. As she centered the clay, the Lord began to speak to her and she simply repeated what He said. Then and there, Master Potter

Ministries was born. Jill took Jeremiah 18:2–5 as the ministry's key verses:

> "Arise and go down to the potter's house, and there I will cause you to hear My words." Then I went down to the potter's house, and there he was, making something at the wheel. And the vessel that he made of clay was marred in the hand of the potter; so he made it again into another vessel, as it seemed good to the potter to make.

RELEASING THE FIRE OF GOD

As the ministry grew, Jill raised up an acting troupe who interpreted the stories she told while creating pieces on the wheel. They began to notice that as they performed, God would come and grip people. Men would weep in each other's arms. Some would get delivered, while others would have open visions. But it didn't happen everywhere. God began to teach Jill why He moved the way He did, and how to cooperate with the Holy Spirit as He moved.

There is a principle in life and in the Scriptures that something first occurs in the natural and then in the spiritual. (See 1 Corinthians 15:46.) That is exactly the way it worked with the beloved Jill Austin. Because Jill worked with kilns as a potter, God began to teach her about His fire. John the Baptist said Jesus would baptize us with the Holy Spirit and with fire (see Matthew 3:11; Luke 3:16), but His is not the fire of destruction—it is the fire that empowers us to be who He created us to be.

Have you ever been in a worship service and felt electrified, as if every cell of your body vibrated in worship to our King? If so, then you've experienced the fire of God in worship. Other times, the glory fire is released when God invades a place with His manifest presence. People begin to see angels and encounter heaven in a way that ruins them for anything else.

The glory fire is released

when God invades a place with

His manifest presence.

After a while, God instructed Jill to lay down her potter's wheel and just preach and release the fire of God. So Jill became a fiery preacher and prophetic minister. Eventually, she joined the prophetic movement in Kansas City at Metro Christian Fellowship. This move coincided with a heavenly sign.

In 1993, Bob Jones, an amazing "fatherly seer prophet" within this highly gifted group, prophesied that there would be a new voice assigned to the movement, and an actual comet in the natural would confirm its arrival. When Jill arrived in Kansas City, the sky was indeed lit up by a comet. Aptly, it was named the Austin Comet. Anyone who ever witnessed Jill ministering would agree it was a perfect metaphor. The raw power released by the Holy Spirit was like a fiery comet colliding with the earthly realm.

Night after night, Jill ministered for hours, desperate for everyone to encounter the raw fire of God. When I ministered alongside her, my role was to sing prophetically on the themes she would call out to me. I remember ministering in meetings with Jill until one and two o'clock in the morning, and each time she would leave asking, "What else could we have done? How could we have helped more people experience Him?" Her consuming desire was to see all His people moving in the power of the Holy Spirit. She wanted every church where she ministered to be not just a place of visitation by the Spirit, but a place truly inhabited by Him.

I could tell countless stories about people encountering the fire of God at Jill's meetings, but one in particular, which I witnessed personally, still amazes me. A young man walked into one of the meetings and was instantaneously lifted off the floor, then slammed to the ground. He wrestled with this unseen force for about three hours. I recall seeing him crawling to the wall to try to pull himself up, only to be snatched right back down.

When he was interviewed later, he said that on the way to the meeting, his friends had asked him if he was afraid to go, knowing he was somewhat rebellious at the time. He had answered, "No.

I've been around some of the top prophetic leaders, Bob Jones and Paul Cain. Nothing ever happens to me." Yet as soon as he entered the room, he felt two large hands grab him around the waist, and he heard a voice whisper in his ear, "I thought you said nothing ever happens to you." That's when he was thrown to the floor—and when he was radically changed.

HEARING "HOLY GHOST STORIES"

Jill modeled dependence on the Holy Spirit like no one I have seen before or since. She had a childlike faith. Willing to risk her own failure and embarrassment and take chances, Jill lived to see Him minister to every individual she encountered. As a woman in ministry, especially one who walked in the level of anointing she had, Jill was a pioneer. She frequently experienced rejection and ridicule for what the Holy Spirit did through her, but she didn't care. She loved Jesus with her whole heart and the Holy Spirit was her Friend. She spoke *to* Him, calling out, "Holy Spirit," rather than *about* Him, saying *"the* Holy Spirit." The simple act of addressing Him by name revealed her level of intimacy with Him.

Jill also had a very accurate prophetic gift born of this intimacy. She spoke razor-sharp truth to individuals and leaders all over the world. She didn't just save it for meetings and formal events. Jill would walk right up to people in the course of everyday life and give them a timely word free from religious jargon so they could understand it and use it right away.

I loved to sit and listen to her "Holy Ghost stories," as she called them. One of my favorites was about the time Jill and the troupe of actors with whom she traveled were on a plane, heading out on a ministry trip. Jill was sitting by the aisle, her friend and team member Naomi was in the middle seat, and a man they didn't know had the window seat. As the plane took off, Jill's eyes met the stranger's.

"You have a spirit of murder on you," she said to him.

"Not now, Jill," Naomi urged.

Jill pressed on. "But he does. He wants to kill his wife."

The guy made a kind of growl.

Unperturbed, Jill continued. "You're also afraid of narcotics agents because you are a cocaine dealer."

I don't know what happened during the rest of the flight, but I do know that when the plane landed, Jill and Naomi had a three-hour layover. Instead of getting away from them as fast as he could, this guy followed them around the airport asking question after question. By the time they made their connecting flight, he'd given his life to Christ. Now isn't that what the true prophetic ministry is supposed to be about? *"The testimony of Jesus is the spirit of prophecy"* (Revelation 19:10).

Another of my favorite stories is about the day Jill had to go to traffic court. (Consider this proof she was still human like the rest of us.) Knowing there was a long, boring day of sitting ahead of her, she showed up prepared to work on correspondence for the ministry. She arranged her work on the desk where she was seated, and everyone else did the same. Just as they were settled, the judge announced, "Everyone needs to clear their desks or they won't get credit for this." You can imagine the collective sighs and grumbles.

Jill remembered thinking, *Oh no, Lord, this is going to be a boring day. Can You just give me words of knowledge for people?*

The Lord began to speak to her about various people in the room. He told her the judge was going through a midlife crisis and had just bought a red sports car. He told her that another guy, also there for traffic court, was a lawyer. Jill thought he looked more like a criminal, but the Lord insisted he was an attorney.

A moment later, the judge asked, "Is there an attorney here?"

Intimacy with God is just the beginning. What He is really after is divine union.

No one responded. The man the Lord had said was an attorney had his head down, clearly not planning to come clean. Jill pointed at him and said, "Well, he is." The judge asked how she knew and she said, "God told me." The judge then asked the man if this was true, and he admitted that yes, he was an attorney.

Later during a break, Jill approached the man.

"Are you a psychic?" he asked.

She said, "No. I love Jesus," and began to prophesy over him. He hung on every word.

If I told all of Jill's Holy Ghost stories, it would take an entire book. Long before anyone had heard of "treasure hunts"—in which you ask God to help you identify specific people to pray for—God used a childlike woman from California to model what it might look like to simply hear God in everyday life and love people with His heart.

"ALL I HAVE IS HIM"

There is so much more I could say about Jill Austin. She was a prophet who saw into the spirit realm. She was an ambassador of the King who moved in the raw power of God. But most of all, she was a daughter of God, a friend of the Holy Spirit, and a lover of Jesus. She will be remembered not just for her incredible exploits, but for the intimacy she had with the King of Kings and Lord of Lords. Her willingness to go and do whatever He told her to do—simply because she loved Him—humbles me. As a single woman in ministry, she moved in places where many men lack the courage to go. And she was never afraid to confront the religious order for shutting down the movement of God.

When asked why the Holy Spirit came so powerfully when she ministered, her response was, "Well, you all have wives or husbands. All I have is Him."

The Lord once said to me that I thought intimacy with Him was the ultimate goal, but He wanted me to understand that intimacy is just the beginning. What He is really after is *divine union.* Jill demonstrated this union with her life of obedience to Him, and I'm deeply honored to call her my spiritual mother. I pray her heart's cry becomes ours: "Lord, all I have is You, and You are more than enough for me." Truly, His presence is the only thing that satisfies. Nothing but more of Him will do.

"UNLESS A GRAIN OF WHEAT FALLS..."

Two weeks before Jill went home to be with the Lord, I heard the Lord saying Jill was not going to be with us much longer. In denial, I told myself it was just me, brushed it off, and didn't think about it anymore. The possibility of Jill's death made no sense to me because I knew she had some big promises yet to be fulfilled. She had great things she wanted to do for God, and like her, I really believed her desires were from Him.

Then, on January 8, 2009, I received a call telling me Jill was in critical condition and I needed to pray. Every time I prayed, I heard John 12:24 in my mind: *"Most assuredly, I say to you, unless a grain of wheat falls into the ground and dies, it remains alone; but if it dies, it produces much grain."*

"Lord, what does it mean?" I asked. I didn't want to accept that I already knew what it meant—the Lord was calling her home. On January 9, at about 7:45 p.m. California time, I had a vision of Jill before the throne of God, her hands lifted as she worshipped her King. I knew she was gone. I later learned that, indeed, Jill had died in Kansas City at 9:48 p.m. on January 9, 2009.

The Lord began to speak to me about John 12:24. He said Jill had fallen into the ground like a seed, and as a result, the anointing that was on her life was about to be released to the body of Christ. All the promises she carried and the works she did would be passed to the next generation. I was reminded of a conversation I'd had with Jill years before while on a flight to a ministry engagement. I don't even remember what we had been discussing, but at one point, she looked at me and said, "André, one day I am going to be in the great cloud of witnesses cheering you on, saying, 'André, go for it! Run with everything in you!'"

As I recalled her words, I began to understand: her baton had been passed to us, and we must now run our part in the race. I have picked up the baton in this relay race and am running my lap with Holy Spirit. Are you?

After Jill died, I dreamed about her on many occasions. In one symbolic dream, I walked into a room and Jill was sitting in a chair. She didn't look up at me, but I started talking to her anyway. I wanted to tell her how sad I was that she had passed. When she did not acknowledge me, I decided to try another tactic, and began telling her of the dream I'd had right after she died. In that dream, I was sitting in the front row of a church. Jill entered the church, walked up to me, and laid hands on me. The anointing was so heavy, it felt as though I was being pressed into the chair. She then walked behind me and sat down. She put her right hand on my right shoulder and sat there for a few minutes. Finally, she said, "You will be fine now. I have to leave." Then she got up and left the room.

In my new dream, as I was telling her about the earlier dream, she interrupted me. "André, what I lived my life for is about to happen," she said. "And whether it was with me or whether it is with you, it does not matter." I then woke up.

I knew immediately what the Lord was saying to me because I knew what Jill had lived for— to see a generation of people encounter the Holy Spirit and embark on the glorious journey of learning to walk with Him in intimacy, dependence, power, and joy. There is a coming outpouring of the Spirit that will be far greater than anything we've ever seen before. And so, in the pages ahead, I offer some of what I have learned about who He is, how He moves, and how we can move with Him. Nothing is worth more than divine union with Him.

2

CARRYING HIS HEART

God has always longed for relationship with His people. Reading the Bible from Genesis to Revelation, we find the story of a God pursuing a people who would simply love Him and come into covenant relationship with Him. Jesus's final prayer for His disciples in John 17 makes this plain as day:

> Now I am no longer in the world, but these are in the world, and I come to You. Holy Father, keep through Your name those whom You have given Me, that they may be one as We are.... I do not pray for these alone, but also for those who will believe in Me through their word; that they all may be one, as You, Father, are in Me, and I in You; that they also may be one in Us, that the world may believe that You sent Me. And the glory which You gave Me I have given them, that they may be one just as We are one: I in them, and You in Me; that they may be made perfect in one, and that the world may know that You have sent Me, and have loved them as You have loved Me. (John 17:11, 20–23)

Jesus lived and died not just to forgive our sin, but so we could become *one* with Him and the Father through the Holy Spirit. Divine union is the heart of the gospel.

"Tell the people I have scanned them," He said. "Tell My people I am pleased with them."

The depth of intimacy and partnership with the Holy Spirit that Jill Austin and other leaders have experienced—people like John Wesley, Charles Finney, William Seymour, John G. Lake, Kathryn Kuhlman, John Wimber, Paul Cain, and Bob Jones—was never meant to belong exclusively to special, "super" Christians. Rather, such men and women are pioneers who have shown the body of Christ what is available for all of us in the realms of the Spirit if we will simply respond to His invitation for intimacy.

What keeps so many people in the church from pursuing intimacy with the Spirit? There are many reasons, but one of the biggest is that the enemy has discouraged people from pursuing God by misrepresenting His heart for them.

KNOWING THE GOD OF THE BIBLE

Once I was sitting in worship getting ready to speak at a conference, asking the Lord what He wanted me to do. Suddenly, I had a vision of a document scanner, though there was no document on it. I thought, *Well, that's interesting*, but had no clue what it meant. I think many of us usually don't understand what the Lord is telling us right away.

Then the Lord spelled it out for me. "Tell the people I have scanned them," He said.

My first thought was fearful. *Uh-oh. God is about to lower the "boom." We are going to get it now.*

But then He said, "Tell My people I am pleased with them."

"Really?" I answered aloud. It felt like a happy surprise to hear these words from the Lord, even though I already knew they were true.

When I got up to share, I described my vision signifying that the Lord had scanned the people. I could feel everyone bracing themselves for the rebuke that was coming, just as I had. I continued: "And the Lord wants me to tell you He is pleased with you." The whole room responded with true adoration of the Lover of their souls.

That experience made me aware that in the over forty years I have known the Lord, the amount of times I have heard sermons preached about God's pleasure in His children is widely disproportionate to the number of sermons I have heard about His anger toward us. It's no wonder most of us feel like we can never measure up, that God is a mean ogre just waiting for us to mess up so He can punish us, and if we make it to heaven, it will be by the skin of our teeth. It's no wonder we struggle to move toward a God like that.

That is *not* the God of the Bible. We have a pressing need for Bible teaching that unravels these misrepresentations and helps us understand, believe, and experience God's true heart toward us. Yes, the Bible clearly reveals that God, because He is good, does not allow wrongdoing to go unpunished. However, the person of Jesus reveals the heart of God to restore sinners to relationship with Him. When the disciples asked Jesus to show them the Father, He said, *"He who has seen Me has seen the Father"* (John 14:9). He is the *"express image"* of the Father (Hebrews 1:3), *"the exact representation of His being"* (verse 3, NIV). His heart is the Father's heart. He sees and feels exactly like the Father sees and feels, so when you read how Jesus responded to a sinner, it was just as the Father was responding. Jesus was called—and is—the Friend of sinners.

God the Father so loved the world that He sent Jesus to bring us back to His arms. The revelation of His love—love that is *"strong as death"* and *"unyielding as the grave"* (Song of Songs 8:6 NIV)—will cause us to run toward Him instead of away from Him.

It's a mistake to think that maintaining a view of God as perpetually punishing will convince people to pursue a holy life. It's

His kindness that leads us to repentance. (See Romans 2:4.) A true encounter with the love of God does not lead us to think, *Now I can go live however I want because God loves me*, but rather, *I don't even want to sin anymore. I don't want anything but Him, and I don't want to do anything that will violate my relationship with Him.* His love leads us into holiness.

THE HEART BEHIND THE GIFTS

It's simple logic that if God's people never receive a revelation of His true heart for them, they will never be able to show that heart to the world. The misrepresentation they accept will be the misrepresentation they display to others. There are a lot of people out there practicing spiritual gifts without the Holy Spirit's heart, and the effects are devastating. We must have character to carry the gifts if we are going to be authentic ambassadors of Christ Jesus.

One time, the Lord gave me a word of knowledge that a young man in my California youth group was struggling with a particular sin. The Lord also made it clear I was not to confront him about the issue, but was simply to love him. Sometimes, the best way to help people is just to love them and pray for them. As this young man was struggling with this sin, in his heart, he was crying out for help. I knew that as long as he continued to come to our group, God would touch and transform him in the corporate anointing. The presence of God is where we receive what we need, where we are changed.

Week after week, this young man continued to come and I could see the Holy Spirit ministering to him. He was growing in his relationship with God. It was awesome to watch the Lord do what He does. I'm convinced that if we would just get out of the way and let God be God, we would see much more fruit in people's lives.

The goal of every believer

should be to see others and

ourselves through the eyes of God.

Eventually, my time with that particular church ended and I followed God's call to a church in New York City, but I stayed in contact with a lot of people in the California youth group. One day I got a call from one of the young men with whom I was close. He wanted to tell me about something distressing that had happened at the church. A prophet had come to minister and had an altar call for people who wanted prayer. The young man I had prayed for was at the meeting and came forward for prayer. The prophet said to him over the microphone, "You're in sexual sin, aren't you?" The young man dropped his head and said, "Yes." Then he walked away. He never returned to the church. To this day, I don't know if he is walking with God.

The young man who called me wanted to know why God would do that to someone. The guy had come up for prayer—it was obvious he was crying out for help. Why would God just destroy him like that?

My response was God would never do that. I told him the prophet may have been trying to show how "prophetic" he was and he sacrificed this guy to do it. I also said he will have to answer to God because of what he did. He forgot to consider God's heart and intentions toward this young man.

My friend was surprised when I told him I had not only known that the young man was in sin, but I also had known which sin. "How?" he wanted to know. I told him God had shown me, but that He'd also shown me His heart toward him, which was why I'd never revealed the sin or approached the young man about it, but rather allowed the Holy Spirit to minister to him.

Frankly, it's easy to see people's bad stuff. Most wear their shame like a garment. It is much harder to see people as God sees them, in their prophetic potential. This should be the goal of every believer—to see others and ourselves through the eyes of God. Only then will we be able to use words of knowledge, prophecy, and other gifts of the Holy Spirit to bring life and build up God's people.

"NEITHER DO I CONDEMN YOU"

Many believers have still not learned the difference between the Holy Spirit's conviction and the enemy's condemnation. Conviction always draws us back to God, while condemnation drives us away from God through shame and fear. If your thoughts are making you want to hide from God, that is not the Holy Spirit! Matthew 12:20 says, *"A bruised reed He will not break, and smoking flax He will not quench."* Though you may be broken and struggling, God sees the intent of your heart and I believe He counts that as action. He will never crush the life out of you or destroy your hope when you trust in Him.

Consider how Jesus dealt with the woman caught in adultery in John 8:2–11. Her accusers tried to use the law to sway Jesus to agree with stoning her to death, but Jesus simply began to write on the ground with His finger. No one really knows what He wrote; I have heard many different theories. Some believe He was writing out the sins of the crowd, or even showing them He knew that some of the very ones who were crying out against her had themselves slept with her. Whatever it was, He told her accusers, *"He who is without sin among you, let him throw a stone at her first"* (John 8:7).

Everyone, starting with the oldest, dropped their stones and walked away. Finally, we see how the Lord—the only One without sin—responded:

> *When Jesus had raised Himself up and saw no one but the woman, He said to her, "Woman, where are those accusers of yours? Has no one condemned you?" She said, "No one, Lord." And Jesus said to her, "Neither do I condemn you; go and sin no more."* (John 8:10–11)

Remember, Jesus is the express image of the Father. How Jesus responded is how the Father was responding—and will respond to us. We can come into the presence of the Lord with a conscience that has been cleaned by the precious blood of Jesus. We can approach Him with confidence:

> Seeing then that we have a great High Priest who has passed through the heavens, Jesus the Son of God, let us hold fast our confession. For we do not have a High Priest who cannot sympathize with our weaknesses, but was in all points tempted as we are, yet without sin. Let us therefore come boldly to the throne of grace, that we may obtain mercy and find grace to help in time of need.　　　　　(Hebrews 4:14–16)

Let us come boldly before the throne of grace. His grace is sufficient for us. (See 2 Corinthians 12:9.) Where sin abounds, grace abounds so much more. (See Romans 5:20.)

JESUS WEEPS OVER THE LOST

If the people of God would discover His true heart and stop misrepresenting Him, I believe so much of the world would finally discover how irresistibly attractive He is. Instead of constantly pointing out what's wrong with the world, or even what's wrong with the church, I pray we would begin to shout His grace over our churches, our cities, and our nations. If we not only shout His grace, but also show it, we will see lives radically changed. It is Satan who always wants us to point out what is wrong; God's heart is to prophesy the opposite spirit. He calls those things that do not exist as though they did. (See Romans 4:17.)

One time, when I was in Toronto, Canada, to minister at a conference with Jill Austin, a movie about the AIDS crisis came on TV. In this film, there were Christians bearing signs saying, "Gays go to hell" and "If you mess with God, He will kill you."

Satan wants us to point out what is wrong; God's heart is to prophesy the opposite spirit.

I began to weep uncontrollably, and at once, I understood these weren't my tears. This was the heart of God—and it was breaking.

The Lord spoke to me, "This is My heart for these people. I am tired of you [the wider body of Christ] misrepresenting Me as a God with a baseball bat waiting to beat people up." He let me know that the Jesus who wins the lost is the One who weeps over them. Jesus longs to gather His people as a hen gathers her chicks under her wings. (See, for example, Matthew 23:37.) The presence of the Lord is a safe place, a place of protection for His people—all His people.

WE ARE BOUND TO HIM

The Lord once said to me, "When you don't understand the way My hand is moving in your life, you've got to understand My heart for you. I will never leave you or forsake you. I have your best interests at heart."

Life holds plenty of mysteries for all of us. Things happen that we don't understand. But *"Jesus Christ is the same yesterday, today, and forever"* (Hebrews 13:8), and He has not changed His heart toward us. This is the one thing we can be sure of—He loves us and will cause everything to work out for our good. (See Romans 8:28.) He is for us and not against us. He will not give up on us or relent in pursuing us. He can be trusted. He is faithful to complete what He started. (See Philippians 1:6.)

The reason we can be so sure of God's faithfulness toward us lies in the nature of the covenant He has made with us in Christ. Through Jesus's incarnation, death, and resurrection, the God of the universe has forever bound Himself to us. We are written on the palms of His hands (see Isaiah 49:16); additionally, every time He sees the nail prints in His hands, He sees us. We have become one flesh and spirit with Him. He has made us His family.

The Holy Spirit is specifically assigned by the Father to make this covenant real to us, to show us He has truly adopted us as His sons and daughters. The Bible says even if your mother and father put you out, He will take you in. (See Psalm 27:10.) I can say from personal experience that this is true. He has been my mother, my father, my brother, and my sister. He has been everything I have ever needed Him to be. He is so faithful! How deep and how wide is the love He has for His children!

Because we are bound in covenant with the Lord, He is always with us. David wrote, *"Where can I flee from Your presence? If I ascend into heaven, You are there; if I make my bed in hell, behold, You are there"* (Psalm 139:7–9). God's heart is to dwell in the midst of His people. Even when we can't feel Him, He is with us. We know this by faith because His Word says He won't leave us. (See, for example, Hebrews 13:5.)

David also instructed us to wait on the Lord and He would strengthen our hearts. (See Psalm 27:14.) In this verse, the Hebrew word for "wait" is *qavah*, which means "to bind yourself to," and the word in Hebrew for "Lord" is *Yehovah*, or *Yahweh*, God's covenant name. When our heart is fainting and we can't seem to find a way out of a situation, we must bind ourselves to the God who keeps covenant with His people. He will strengthen our hearts and make every crooked place straight. (See Isaiah 45:2.) Because He can't fail, there is no need to stress out about the situation. God's got it all under control.

HE REJOICES OVER US

The more the Holy Spirit reveals the heart of the Father to us, the more convinced we will become that God is not only faithful and present with us—He is truly pleased with us! He delights in us as a good father delights in his children. He rejoices over us with singing:

> *In that day it shall be said to Jerusalem: "Do not fear.... The Lord your God in your midst, the Mighty One, will save; He*

will rejoice over you with gladness, He will quiet you with His love, He will rejoice over you with singing."
(Zephaniah 3:16–17)

These verses hold great meaning for me and are among my life verses. Often when I am singing on the worship team, I will pray these verses. "Lord," I will say, "You said You rejoice over us with singing. Let me hear the song You are singing over the people right now." I stop and listen, and then I repeat what I hear. I have heard testimony after testimony of people who said the prophetic song pierced their hearts with the love of God. They had wondered if God knew or even cared about their situations, but after hearing the song He was singing over them, they left knowing that He did.

Interestingly, our DNA actually equates to musical notation. In other words, scientists can take your DNA and convert it to music.[1] They can literally play your song. Therefore, when the presence of the Lord comes and His song is released over a person, the song that they are, down to the cellular level, begins to line up and reverberate with the song of the Lord being sung over them. This beautiful melody releases life in them. Broken hearts and bodies are healed. A woman recently wrote and told me that several of her physical ailments had been healed due to prophetic singing. What if all we need to heal, as the old saying goes, is a "double dose of the Holy Ghost"?

In Hebrew, *rejoice* can signify to twirl about. So in these verses from Zephaniah, the Lord is saying He not only sings a love song over you, but when you come into His presence, He also begins to dance. Imagine that! The King of the universe, the same God who said, *"Let there be light"* (Genesis 1:3) loves you so much that when you enter His presence, He begins to dance over you. And then He bursts into song.

---

1. https://www.cbsnews.com/news/dna-makes-sweet-music (accessed June 18, 2018)

God loves you so much that

when you enter His presence,

He begins to dance over you.

And then He bursts into song.

In the words of my friend and prophetic psalmist JoAnn McFatter, "What are you going to do with a God like that?" When we truly see and experience God's heart toward us, we can have only one response. Like Mary of Bethany, who poured out her most precious possession, costly oil, perhaps her bridal dowry, on Jesus (see John 11:2), we must give all we have out of love for the One who loves us completely. Surrendering our lives to Him is simply the obvious thing to do when we encounter His love. This is the goal of my life. I want to live my life as a drink offering before the Lord. How about you? (See, for example, Genesis 35:14; Romans 12:1.)

ALLOW HIM TO HEAL YOUR HEART

I encourage you to invite the Holy Spirit to show you the heart the Father has for you. Ask Him to expose any misrepresentation of God that you have believed and replace it with the truth of who He is. Allow Him to heal your heart of all condemnation and shame and ask Him to reveal to you how He sees you. May you encounter Him with His incredible, passionate love for you, and may He plant deeply in your heart the truth that nothing can separate you from His love. May His love transform you so you become a living encounter with the heart of God for every person you meet.

3

WHEN THE BREAKER COMES

The Holy Spirit has a very clear assignment and agenda in our lives. He is here to make sure Jesus gets what He paid for—a family of restored sons and daughters who know who they are and *whose* they are, who carry His heart, and who are partnering with Him to see His kingdom come on earth. For this reason, every lie, bondage, or obstacle that would keep us from becoming the fullness of Jesus's inheritance is a target for the Holy Spirit. He is the Spirit of liberty who comes to set us free to know and love God, and become who He created us to be.

When Jesus began His ministry, He announced that He had been given an anointing of the Holy Spirit to set people free, *"to proclaim freedom for the prisoners and recovery of sight for the blind, to set the oppressed free"* (Luke 4:18 NIV). Another name for this anointing is the "breaker" anointing, which is based in part on Isaiah 10:27: *"It shall come to pass in that day that his burden will be taken away from your shoulder, and his yoke from your neck, and **the yoke will be destroyed** ["broken" NIV] **because of the anointing oil."** The yoke is a symbol of alignment and partnership. The breaker anointing of the Holy Spirit comes to shatter every point of agreement and partnership that we might have with the devil and the powers of darkness in our lives, and remove the heavy burdens and bondages they create. This frees us to align, agree, and partner with Him—the One whose yoke is easy and whose burden is light. (See Matthew 11:30.) And as the Holy Spirit sets us free and teaches us to walk in freedom, He also invites us to release His breaker anointing to set others free.

THE BREAKER ANOINTING

In the fall of 2002, the Lord began to speak to me about the breaker anointing of the Holy Spirit. At the time, I was living in Minneapolis and joining Jill on the road for ministry when I could. I had frequently heard people say this or that person "has the breaker anointing," but the term had never been explained to me. I knew enough to realize I had experienced it through Jill's ministry, and people had told me I had it as well, but I really didn't have language yet to explain it.

The Lord took me on a journey of discovery. He began to "download" Scripture to me, which the Holy Spirit would explain. One day during this time, I had what I like to call a mini-visitation in my apartment. (A visitation occurs when the Lord comes into your space and time. Basically, it means God has chosen to powerfully reveal Himself to you. Such visitations take various forms.) The presence of the Lord suddenly became uniquely tangible. I could feel the presence of angels moving through the room (see Hebrews 1:7, 14) and saw what appeared to be smoke filling the air. It was as if heaven had invaded my apartment with His manifest presence. I knew I was doing what God wanted me to do and there was something about the breaker anointing He wanted to release.

The Lord highlighted Micah 2:13 to me: *"The one who breaks open will come up before them; they will break out, pass through the gate, and go out by it; their king will pass before them, with the LORD at their head."* The Hebrew word translated "breaks open" and "break out" is *parats*; among its meanings is "to break open, to burst forth, or to come out." The breaker anointing of the Spirit breaks open the heavens and removes blockages that have been preventing the presence of God from moving in its fullness. It confronts not only the bondages and issues in our individual lives, but also the dark spiritual forces that preside over cities, regions, and nations.

For example, when the Holy Spirit was poured out on the day of Pentecost, He broke open the heavens over Jerusalem, removing the spiritual barriers keeping people from receiving the gospel. Thousands of people from every culture and language were saved in one day due to that outpouring. (See Acts 2:1–41.) The breaker anointing removed the veil over the eyes of people, so that which was once hidden in darkness suddenly came into the light.

Let's explore what the breaker anointing looks like with a story from Jill's ministry and one of my own experiences.

"DANCE WITH MY ANGELS"

In the early nineties, Jill was invited to minister at a church in Christchurch, New Zealand. During the first meeting, the Lord moved with great power. Many were touched by His awesome presence that night. Afterward, she went back to the home of the pastor who was hosting her to get some rest.

In the middle of the night, the Lord woke her up and asked, "Do you want to dance with My angels?"

"Are they at the church?" Jill asked.

"No," He said, "they are downstairs in the living room."

Exhausted from the meeting, Jill respectfully declined the invitation. Afterward, she always said she wished she had gone down to the living room that night.

When she arrived at the church the next evening, the atmosphere was even more powerful. It was simply charged with God. Wave after wave of God's glory invaded the room. I remember her describing the glory as so tangible that you could walk through the room and dip your hand into it. She said it was like liquid gold on your hands—you could actually see it. The church had metal chairs and whenever a wave of God's presence came, they would crash to the ground as people fell on them. People were not hurt one bit—they were healed, delivered, and set free. Revival began to visit the city and the nation. Jill recalled how they would try to leave the building after the meetings were over, but couldn't because of the intensity of the angelic presence. I guess the angels still wanted to dance.

What started in Christchurch began to spread throughout much of New Zealand and later into Australia. In Australia, fire literally appeared on top of churches where revival was breaking out. Fire trucks came, but there was no natural fire for them to extinguish—it was the tangible fire of God. (See, for example, Acts 2.) The effects of God's movement are still being felt in those two nations to this day.

FORGIVENESS FOR GRAND FORKS

In January 2002, Bruce Allen, a prophet and a good friend, went with me to Grand Forks, British Columbia, for a New Year's prophetic conference. Grand Forks is a picturesque, quaint little town, but when I entered the city, I couldn't help noticing that it seemed to be dying. Business after business had shut down and there were no signs of any new industry.

Bruce spoke the first night and I have to admit, I was really glad I wasn't the one speaking. Have you ever felt like you were hitting a brick wall? You have tried everything you know to do, but there is just no breakthrough. This meeting felt like that times a thousand. I knew Bruce was thinking, *What is going on?* I was wondering the same thing. He finally asked me, "You got anything?"

I shrugged my shoulders as I often do when I am stumped. "No," I said. I decided I should probably ask the Lord what was going on. (You've got to forgive me—sometimes I am kind of slow on the uptake.)

The Lord responded rather quickly. "It is because of what happened to the Native Americans here," He said. "There is a curse on the land."

I said, "Lord, what Native Americans? Everybody here just looks like normal, everyday white people to me."

He didn't say anything else, so after the meeting, I decided to ask the pastor about it. "What happened to the Native Americans here?"

"Why do you ask?" he replied.

I explained that the Lord had told me there was a curse on the land because of what had happened to them.

"Well," he said, "they were basically slaughtered on the land where the church is built." Custer's army, he told me, had driven the Native Americans across the border into Canada. They had lived there peaceably for three years and then the army decided to come over and murder them in their sleep.

The next day, I met with an intercessor, a strong prayer warrior who did spiritual mapping by studying history while also employing the gift of discerning of spirits. He told me the Lord had tried to release revival in the city many times, but the leaders of some of the churches had said no to the move of God. He said it was as if the gatekeepers of the city had stood at the gates and said, "Sorry, God. We don't want You here."

After the intercessor left, I went before the Lord to ask Him what He wanted me to do, as it was my turn to speak that night. He said I should release identification repentance. (Identification repentance is simply confessing the generational sins of someone else or an entire people group and asking for forgiveness on their

*The Holy Spirit causes us
to see what is important and
equips us with strategies to bring
that vision to pass.*

behalf. It's what Daniel did when interceding for Israel, as recorded in Daniel 7–9.)

That night at the meeting, I asked if anyone present had Native American ancestry. To my surprise, fifteen people came forward. There were only about forty people in attendance, so fifteen was quite a large percentage. God really had my attention at that point.

Next, I called up ministry leaders from the region and asked them to face the Native Americans. I asked them to repent to the Native Americans for what had happened to their ancestors. I then asked the Native Americans if they would forgive the atrocities inflicted upon them. Through tears, they said, "Yes. We will."

Finally, I asked the leaders to repent for keeping the move of God out of the region. Bruce later told me that as they repented, he heard a scream in the spirit realm. He said it was as if the dark, demonic principality holding back the move of God knew its power over the region was broken.

Additionally, during the meeting, woman who was a seer-type prophet announced she had seen the spiritual gates of the city swing open. Then, she saw the angel of revival who had been kept outside the gate fly in and stand next to me. Suddenly, the Lord began to move with power.

Some time after those meetings in Grand Forks, I learned that revival had broken out in the church. For a period of time, healing and miracles became normal occurrences and people's hearts were turned back to the Lord. The mayor and his wife both ended up getting saved and industry started moving back into the region.

REVELATION AND AGREEMENT

As you can see from these stories, operating in the breaker anointing is all about listening and responding to the Holy Spirit. He is the One who knows how to bring freedom by realigning us with His truth and purpose.

> *He* [man] *breaks open* [parats] *a shaft away from people; in places forgotten by feet they hang far away from men; they swing to and fro.*   (Job 28:4)

The Holy Spirit makes a place even where people have forgotten to walk. In life's journey, it's easy to get sidetracked by daily cares and forget our purpose—the reason we were created. When that happens, He comes as the Breaker and draws us back to what is important. He calls us to those things of eternal value. He causes us to see what is important and equips us with strategies to bring that vision to pass.

Ultimately, all He is asking is that we agree with Him. When the Breaker comes and removes our spiritual blindness so we can see the hand of God at work, we naturally fall into the agreement He desires. Whenever you are in agreement with someone, power is released into the relationship. So, when you come into agreement with heaven, heaven is released in and through you.

THE INTERCESSOR AND THE BREAKER

One biblical example of how the Holy Spirit brought the people of God back into alignment with Him is found in the story of Samuel. First Samuel 3:1 also uses the Hebrew word *parats*, translating it "widespread." It says, *"Now the boy Samuel ministered to the* LORD *before Eli. And the word of the* LORD *was rare in those days; there was no widespread revelation."* This verse might be translated, "There was no breaker anointing to release revelation."

Eli was the high priest, appointed to walk in the breaker anointing that would release revelation to the people. However, Eli's sons chose to live in rebellion and Eli chose to turn a blind eye. The man called by God to uphold righteousness allowed sin to gain a stronghold in his own household and thus his ears became dull to the voice of the Lord. The word of the Lord was only rare in those days because man stopped listening, not because God stopped speaking. So God had to raise up another man who would listen to His voice: Samuel.

The Bible introduces us to Samuel's mother first, for a reason. Hannah was a forerunner of a generation of people today who will not give the Lord any rest until His kingdom is established in the earth as He has purposed, until there is a sustained move of God that will last until Jesus returns, until the church is no longer a laughingstock to the world, and until the glory of the Lord is revealed in her like never before. Hannah's prayers prepared the way for her spiritual breakthrough. She prayed so fervently at the temple, Eli thought she was drunk. (See 1 Samuel 1:13.)

I'm sure she looked very strange, but I'm also sure she didn't care what anybody thought. She desperately wanted a child. She believed God for a son and promised the Lord that if He gave her one, she would dedicate him to God for his entire life. She was an intercessor who would not give up until she got the word from the Lord that it was done. God answered Hannah's prayers and Hannah kept her word. When the child was old enough, she took him to the temple and left him in Eli's care to serve the Lord. It strikes me that the Scripture says when Samuel was a child, he *"ministered to the LORD"* (1 Samuel 2:11). He had it right—our first ministry is to the Lord.

Before we can give anything to others, we first have to spend time gazing upon Him. Through Hannah's faithfulness and Samuel's dedication, God used Samuel as a forerunner or breaker. He became the catalyst for the heavens to open up and release the voice of the Lord over the earth again.

WHO WILL PAY THE PRICE?

In my study of the breaker anointing, the Lord also spoke to me about Ezekiel 22:30: *"So I sought for a man among them who would make a wall, and stand in the gap before Me on behalf of the land, that I should not destroy it; but I found no one."* The word translated "gap" is *perets*, which comes from the root *parats*, which, as we know, can mean "to break open" or to "break out." However, *perets* carries a slightly different meaning: "breaking forth."

God is saying He is looking for a people who will create an atmosphere for Him to move. He longs not to be contained in the four walls of the church. He wants to break out, to affect whole cities and regions. He is raising up a people anointed by the Holy Spirit who know how to hold the heavens open for the "more" of God to come. They will come together to contend for the move of God. Like Hannah, they will cry out, "We won't back down and we won't give up." They will shout, *"Lift up your heads, O you gates! And be lifted up, you everlasting doors! And the King of glory shall come in"* (Psalm 24:7).

God is calling for pioneers who will not settle for second-class Christianity, but who will declare to the enemy, "Enough is enough. We are not resting until we see the glory of the Lord cover the earth as the waters cover the sea!" (See Habakkuk 2:14.)

When I am ministering, I often hear the Lord ask, "Where are My burning ones? Where are the ones who burn with passion for the Son of God?" There is an invitation for us to come into the chamber of the King and receive this powerful anointing for breakthrough. How many are really willing to pay the price, to break through and be real agents of change in the earth? While salvation is free, His anointing is very costly—it will cost you everything. But what you get from Him will be of so much more value than the "everything" you give up. An old gospel song by Doris Mae Akers said it best: "You can't beat God's giving, no matter how hard you try."

So let us say, "Yes, Lord! Release the breaker anointing! Kingdom, come *now*. Thy will be done *now* on earth as it is in heaven, for Jesus Christ's sake. Amen!"

4

ENCOUNTERING HIS GLORY

It's pointing out the obvious to say the Holy Spirit is *holy* and calls us to be holy. But many of us in the body of Christ still don't really have a deep grasp of what holiness is. We continue to look at holiness from an old-covenant mentality, equating it with religious performance and moral perfection, and believing that no matter how much we strive, we can never really attain it. One of the central ministries of the Holy Spirit in our lives is to teach us the beauty of holiness—His holiness and our holiness in Him. (See 1 Chronicles 16:29; 2 Chronicles 20:21.)

WORSHIPPING FOR ALL ETERNITY

Revelation 4 gives us an amazing revelation of how God's holiness affects us when we truly behold it:

After these things I looked, and behold, a door standing open in heaven. And the first voice which I heard was like a trumpet speaking with me, saying, "Come up here, and I will show you things which must take place after this." Immediately I was in the Spirit; and behold, a throne set in heaven, and One sat on the throne. And He who sat there was like a jasper and a sardius stone in appearance; and there was a rainbow around the throne, in appearance like an emerald. Around

*the throne were twenty-four thrones, and on the thrones I saw
twenty-four elders sitting, clothed in white robes; and they
had crowns of gold on their heads. And from the throne pro-
ceeded lightnings, thunderings, and voices. Seven lamps of fire
were burning before the throne, which are the seven Spirits of
God. Before the throne there was a sea of glass, like crystal.
And in the midst of the throne, and around the throne, were
four living creatures full of eyes in front and in back. The first
living creature was like a lion, the second living creature like
a calf, the third living creature had a face like a man, and the
fourth living creature was like a flying eagle. The four living
creatures, each having six wings, were full of eyes around and
within. And they do not rest day or night, saying: "Holy, holy,
holy, Lord God Almighty, who was and is and is to come!"
Whenever the living creatures give glory and honor and
thanks to Him who sits on the throne, who lives forever and
ever, the twenty-four elders fall down before Him who sits on
the throne and worship Him who lives forever and ever, and
cast their crowns before the throne, saying: "You are worthy,
O Lord, to receive glory and honor and power; for You created
all things, and by Your will they exist and were created."*

(Revelation 4:1–11)

The Lord spoke to me once as I pondered this passage, saying
anyone who finds it hard to worship here on earth will not enjoy
heaven much because that's what is happening continually in
heaven. He also said if we find it hard to worship Him here, it
means we *don't really know Him.*

In response, I asked, "But Lord, how much crying and falling
can we do? I mean, I can imagine the first thousand years in heaven
will be pretty exciting, but won't that get old after a while?" (If this
question shocks you a little, please understand something from my
background—I didn't meet my earthly father until I was sixteen
years old. God is the One who has actually fathered me my whole

life. Because I've known Him relationally for so long, I am very comfortable in being honest with Him.)

He said, "André, you don't get it."

"I'm sure I don't," I said. "Would You explain it to me?"

"You have got to understand that each time the four living creatures cry, 'Holy,' I release a fresh revelation of who I Am, of My glory," the Lord explained. "Then the elders exclaim, 'He really is holy!' and again they fall prostrate before Me."

God's holiness is glorious. When you look for *glory* in the dictionary, you find terms like *great honor, renown, praise, distinction, magnificence,* and *great beauty.* God is incomparably and incomprehensively beautiful. He is utterly attractive. And endlessly beholding, enjoying, admiring, and worshipping Him in the beauty of His holiness is what we were created for. The more we discover and experience this, the more we will know beyond a doubt that nothing else will satisfy our hearts. Nothing could be more "heavenly" for us than spending an eternity receiving the revelation of His beautiful glory and holiness.

That is why He commanded us not to make any images to represent Him for our worship. (See Exodus 20:4–5.) Anything we could possibly make, no matter how magnificent, would pale in comparison to the majesty of who He is. I've seen wonderful manifestations of His presence, like gold and emerald dust and even diamonds falling seemingly from nowhere during a time of worship. But as awe-inspiring as all of that was, the Lord tells me it is nothing—nothing!—compared to what awaits us. I've seen just enough to know we have nothing to worry about. Worshipping Him in heaven will *never* get old.

SHAKING THE DOORPOSTS

In the meantime, the Holy Spirit—the Spirit of revelation—wants to open our eyes and hearts to heavenly reality so we will fall

The glory of the Lord causes

creation to tremble at His presence.

in love with His holiness. As I said in the last chapter, the Holy
Spirit is intent on removing our spiritual blindness. Consider how
He opened the eyes of the prophet Isaiah:

> *In the year that King Uzziah died, I saw the Lord sitting on
> a throne, high and lifted up, and the train of His robe filled
> the temple. Above it stood seraphim; each one had six wings:
> with two he covered his face, with two he covered his feet, and
> with two he flew. And one cried to another and said: "Holy,
> holy, holy, is the Lord of hosts; the whole earth is full of His
> glory!" And the posts of the door were shaken by the voice of
> him who cried out, and the house was filled with smoke.*
>
> (Isaiah 6:1–4)

To me, this passage reveals Isaiah's humanity. I've always wondered why it was in the year King Uzziah died that Isaiah saw the
Lord "*high and lifted up.*" I can't prove this biblically, but I imagine
one reason could be that Isaiah had held King Uzziah in a place
only God should occupy. Once that was moved out of the way, the
glory of God was open to Isaiah. When he gazed at the glorious
beauty of the King of Kings, Isaiah was completely undone.

The glory of the Lord causes creation to tremble at His presence. The Hebrew word translated "shaken" in this passage is
nuwa, which means, among other things, "to move back and forth
or tremble." In Acts 4:31, the building where the disciples prayed
literally shook when God's glory filled the room. Actually, the
Greek word used there can mean "to topple over."

My heart's desire is that we all have an Isaiah 6:1 experience.
I pray we will allow the Holy Spirit to pinpoint the things in our
lives that are dimming our view of the Lord and then allow Him
to remove them so we can be completely undone by God's beauty.
I long for the glory of God to cause the doorposts of our hearts to
shake, just like it did the doorposts in the temple.

THE GOD WHO GETS IN YOUR FACE

God's ultimate plan is not just for His people to see His glory and holiness, but for the world to see His glory and holiness through us! In 2 Corinthians, Paul tells us the Holy Spirit is removing the veils that keep us from beholding God's glory, so that by beholding Him, we become transformed into His image. (See 2 Corinthians 3:18.) Through this transformation, we become the revelation of God's glory and holiness on the earth, just as Isaiah prophesied:

> *Arise, shine; for your light has come! And the glory of the*
> Lord *is risen upon you. For behold, the darkness shall cover*
> *the earth, and deep darkness the people; but the* Lord *will*
> *arise over you, and His glory will be seen upon you.*
>
> (Isaiah 60:1–2)

There are two words in Hebrew for glory that I want to point out to suggest two ways people may experience "*beholding...the glory of the Lord*" (2 Corinthians 3:18).

The first is *kabod*, which means His weighty presence, His splendor, and His honor. In many of the meetings in which I minister, you can often feel the weight of God's presence come into the room. People sometimes spontaneously kneel or prostrate themselves before Him. His splendor captivates and everything else fades away. All one can do is worship Him.

Another Hebrew word for glory is *hode*, which means "grandeur, an imposing form and appearance, beauty, comeliness, excellency, honor, and majesty." When the glory of the Lord comes like this, it is as if God steps into your personal space. I like to say He's "the God who gets in your face" with His imposing grandeur. I believe it is in those times that the fear of the Lord is released.

The fear of the LORD is the beginning of wisdom, and the knowledge of the Holy One is understanding.

(Proverbs 9:10)

This is not to say that we should be terrified of God, fearing that if we make a mistake, He'll squash us like a bug. The fear of the Lord is a reverential respect for who He is, expressed by giving Him the honor He is due. In my opinion, many believers have lost that respect. The Lord once said to me that we are constantly asking for revival, and the revival He is going to send is a revival of the fear of the Lord.

His "in-your-face" glory will not give us "warm fuzzies." It will challenge mindsets and draw lines in the sand for us to cross in any area where we are not fully aligned with His lordship. A cause-and-effect power shift occurs when God releases His glory. He imposes Himself on the body of Christ and says, "Ready or not, here I come." Just like the man who appeared before Joshua as *"Commander of the army of the LORD"* (see Joshua 5:13–14), He will not come to choose a side; He'll come to take over.

When God reveals His glory, everything becomes charged with His presence and everything else must fall away. He breaks the back of the religious spirit. He tears down the powerless traditions of men. Things we have established that are not of His design, He will destroy. He says He is going to take back the reins. His will, He says, *will* be done *in us* as it is in heaven.

A few years ago, I had a dream that I believe foretold of this intention. I was standing in a field when a violent wind began to blow. It was so strong, I literally had to grab on to a tree to keep from being blown away. As the wind blew, layer after layer of soil was stripped away. Eventually, the only thing left was bedrock.

I awoke from the dream and the presence of the Lord filled my room. He said, "Grab a pen and a piece of paper and write this down." He told me He is going to release His glory in such a way that it will blow away all the fluff. When He is done, the only thing that will remain is what was built on His name.

He's coming to break us out of the boxes in which we've so carefully placed ourselves. He is stepping into time and invading our space. God is serious about the church walking into her destiny. He is commissioning the sold-out—those who are full of zeal for the Lord. He is stirring the sleeping giant, the church, and rousing her to action, declaring *now* as the time for her to step into her rightful place.

"Enough is enough," He is saying. "The time for just going through the motions is over. It is time for you to grow up."

We grow up by allowing the Holy Spirit to stretch us. This can be painful, as we step out of our comfort zones. I always say faith is spelled "r-i-s-k." We have to decide we want Him more than anything else—more than safety, more than comfort. He created us to be instruments of societal change. This has always been His desire and His will for us. Now, He is ready for us to step up and deliver.

BE TRANSFORMED BY HIS GLORY

Hebrews 10:14 says Jesus has forever perfected those who are being saved. Our job is to allow the sanctifying process to have its full effect. The Holy Spirit is asking us, "Will you allow Me to transform you into My image?"

And rest assured, we must be transformed. The day is coming when every knee will bow and every tongue confess that Jesus Christ is Lord and He is just. (See Philippians 2:10–11.) The book of Revelation says when Jesus comes, many will cry out for the rocks to fall on them and hide them from the face of the One who sits on the throne. (See Revelation 6:15–17.) Why? Because He is going to reveal His glory like never before. If we have not made the necessary preparations, we will not be able to stand in the day of His power.

We must get rid of that which distracts us, maintain our focus on Him, and position ourselves to receive. We must establish and maintain intimacy with Him. He wants us to fully expect Him to do what He has promised. He doesn't want us to be satisfied with what we've experienced; He wants us forever desiring more of Him.

The glory of the Lord is increasing on the earth. Soon, the knowledge of the glory of the Lord is going to cover the earth as the waters cover the sea. Let us prepare ourselves for the greatest release of glory this world has ever seen. I invite you to pray with me:

Lord, I am messed up and I'm with a bunch of messed-up people, but if You can use me, I'll go wherever You want me to go. I'll do whatever You want me to do, because I love You and You are worth it. Amen.

5

DAVID'S TABERNACLE RESTORED

The 24/7 prayer and worship movements that have appeared throughout history—from the disciples in Jerusalem after the crucifixion to the Moravian believers of Europe in the 1700s to today's International House of Prayer in Kansas City, Missouri, (IHOP-KC)—all seek to align the focus and activity of God's people on earth with what is happening in heaven. This is certainly at the heart of the current move and outpouring of the Holy Spirit. He is not only preparing us to worship eternally in heaven; He is bringing the worship of heaven to earth!

However, it's important to understand how this is connected to His mission of training and empowering us to extend the kingdom beyond the walls of any church building and make disciples of all nations. (See Matthew 28:19.) We find this connection expressed in Scripture through the progressive revelation of the tabernacle of David.

Much has been said about the tabernacle in other teachings, but let's briefly cover the relevant passages here.

DAVID BRINGS THE ARK TO THE CITY

David built his tabernacle as a second home for the ark of the covenant—the seat of God's presence among His people. When he

The separation between us and God, caused by the sin of Adam, was utterly destroyed by the sacrifice of Jesus.

attempted to bring the ark to Jerusalem, however, he didn't follow the Lord's instructions to have it carried on the priests' shoulders. David and all the people played music and worshipped the Lord, but the ark was placed on an ox cart. Thus, the foundation of the worship was out of order. When the oxen carrying the ark got to a threshing floor, they stumbled. It looked like the ark was going to fall, so Uzzah, one of the cart's drivers, reached out to steady it and was instantly struck dead. Afraid of the Lord, David decided to leave the ark at the home of Obed-Edom. (See 2 Samuel 6:1–11.)

Some time later, after hearing how God was blessing Obed-Edom, David realized the ark of God was not just for Obed-Edom, but for all people. So he decided to carry the ark back to Jerusalem after all—this time, on the shoulders of the priests as God had prescribed:

> So David went and brought up the ark of God from the house of Obed-Edom to the City of David with gladness. And so it was, when those bearing the ark of the LORD had gone six paces, that he sacrificed oxen and fatted sheep. Then David danced before the LORD with all his might; and David was wearing a linen ephod. So David and all the house of Israel brought up the ark of the LORD with shouting and with the sound of the trumpet.... So they brought the ark of the LORD, and set it in its place in the midst of the tabernacle that David had erected for it. Then David offered burnt offerings and peace offerings before the LORD. (2 Samuel 6:12–15, 17)

After the ark's arrival in the city, David put it in the place he had prepared and established a way of worshipping God that was very different from what took place in the tabernacle of Moses. In Moses's tabernacle, the presence of the Lord was hidden from the common people. Only the high priest—and even he only once a year—could stand before the ark and experience God's glorious presence. But in David's tabernacle, the presence of the Lord was for everyone to experience.

David had a revelation that I don't believe anyone else at the time received. He was like a new covenant man living in the time of the old covenant's rules and regulations. He alone understood that God's presence was not meant to be contained in just one place or experienced by only a special, select few. David recognized that the ultimate goal of the Lord was for His glory to invade the whole earth and for everyone to experience Him. All of us were created to be enjoyed by God and to enjoy His presence.

The sacrifice of praise was offered continually around the ark, with prophetic worship constantly being released. (See 1 Chronicles 16:4–6, 37–38.) This is a beautiful preview and picture of the new covenant. When Jesus died on the cross, His sacrifice satisfied the payment for sin once and for all. That is why the veil separating the Holy Place from the Holy of Holies was torn from top to bottom, both physically in the temple in Jerusalem and spiritually in the heavens. (See, for example, Matthew 27:50–51.) The separation between us and God, caused by the sin of Adam, was utterly destroyed by the sacrifice of the Last Adam, the Lord Jesus Christ. As a result, we have free access, 24/7, into the glorious presence of the living God. David understood this was God's ultimate intention and he took full advantage of it in his day.

THE TABERNACLE RAISED UP

Centuries after David's reign, the prophet Amos prophesied that the Lord would restore the tabernacle of David:

> "On that day I will raise up the tabernacle of David, which has fallen down, and repair its damages; I will raise up its ruins, and rebuild it as in the days of old; that they may possess the remnant of Edom, and all the Gentiles who are called by

My name," says the LORD *who does this thing.*

(Amos 9:11–12)

In order to understand the importance of this verse, one must first understand who Edom is. The Edomites were the descendants of Esau, brother of Jacob, whose main claim to fame was giving away his birthright for a bowl of lentil stew. Let's also remember that Jacob tricked his father into giving him the blessing Esau, the firstborn son, was to receive. (See Genesis 25:30–34; 27:1–40.)

In Romans 9:13, the Lord said, *"Jacob have I loved, but Esau have I hated."* I remember reading that for the first time and saying, "Lord, that seems kind of harsh. Why did You hate Esau? Those are really strong words. And why did You love Jacob? He was a thief! I mean, his very name means *usurper.*"

The Lord explained that Esau cared so little about the birthright—which ultimately was the promise that the Messiah, Redeemer of the world, would come through his lineage—that he gave it away for food. His fleshly needs were of a higher value to him than the promise of the Lord.

Esau is the picture of many of us—even all of us, at one time or another. We care too little about the things of God and only have a temporal understanding of the world. We choose to major in that which has no eternal value. God hates that because it separates us from our purpose in Him. As for Jacob, while God did not condone his deceptive actions, He did love his heart. He loved that Jacob was willing to do whatever it took to receive the birthright.

HUNGRY FOR THE SUPERNATURAL

Amos prophesied that God would raise up the tabernacle of David so those who formerly scorned His blessing and those who have never known His blessing could both experience it at last.

And this is exactly what has happened. In Acts 15:16–17 , at the great Jerusalem council, James quoted this passage from Amos as the explanation for how the Holy Spirit was moving among the Gentiles and bringing them into the family of God through belief in Jesus Christ. People suddenly had access to the presence of God who had never had it before and it was radically changing them. In the same way today, something about David's tabernacle will take the blinders off the people—even those who are like Esau and care more for the here and now than for anything with eternal value. I believe that "something" is nothing less than the key to worldwide revolution—and that is the power of God's presence.

God created us to desire His presence, which, I believe, is why the world is so hungry for the supernatural. If we can't find the genuine, we will settle for the counterfeit. Take a look at the TV shows and films currently flooding popular culture. Mediums and psychics on television, and movies about paranormal activity, witches, and vampires, and a plethora of other supernatural depictions are being released. Similar material is being presented in print and electronic books. As believers, we should not be intimidated by this trend. Instead, it should cause us to take action. If people think they've seen the ultimate in supernatural power, then as the church, we have not done a very good job of representing the power of God's presence to the world.

OPERATING OUT OF AN OPEN HEAVEN

In this very hour, God is restoring the tabernacle of David on the earth. You can see it in places like the International House of Prayer, where worship and intercession are the focus. It is also happening in places like Bethel Church in Redding, California, where they focus on releasing the kingdom of God on earth through signs and wonders. Different aspects of David's tabernacle are being released as these churches and others like them are causing the presence of the Lord to increase on the earth.

The following story is, to me, a perfect example of David's tabernacle being released. It happened a few years ago at the Twin Cities Prophetic Conference in Minnesota. Craig and Suzy Nelson and their team did a great job of getting the word out about the conference, so quite a few people who had never experienced the prophetic movement attended. Many testified they didn't even know what a prophetic conference was, but the Lord had lured them in.

From the very beginning, we knew there was something different about this gathering. There was a level of expectancy I had not experienced for quite some time in the US. The presence of the Lord was tangible. At times during the worship, it seemed as if the roof lifted off of the building and God's throne entered the room. You could feel the presence of angels moving throughout the gathering. Eventually, the most incredible things began to happen. People were being healed simply by the power of His presence. I am very grateful for gifted people and have often witnessed the abilities God gives them, but these healings were not accomplished by anyone moving in their spiritual gifts. This was God Himself coming down and simply being who He is. We weren't operating only out of an anointing; we were operating out of an open heaven.

One significant testimony from the conference was from a lady with severe scoliosis who'd had several operations on her spine. She had rods in her back that prohibited her from bending over and left her in constant pain. In the midst of worship, God began to touch her. A couple of people noticed what was happening and began to bless what God was doing. They brought her to the platform and she testified by bending over and touching her toes. Either God dissolved the metal rods or He made them pliable. Either way, she was totally healed.

Many left the conference testifying that they had never experienced God's presence like that before. Some who had not even

As we enter into His presence with thanksgiving in our hearts, God moves with power.

believed in this kind of thing left exclaiming, "This is real!" What TV show or movie can compare to that?

THE KEY OF DAVID

Isaiah prophesied this of Christ:

The key of the house of David I will lay on his shoulder; so he shall open, and no one shall shut; and he shall shut, and no one shall open. I will fasten him as a peg in a secure place, and he will become a glorious throne to his father's house.

(Isaiah 22:22–23)

I believe the key of David and the tabernacle of David are one and the same. The key is the revelation he had about the presence of the Lord. And for us, a revelation of the presence of the Lord is the fuel that will sustain long-term revival. As we enter into His presence with thanksgiving in our hearts and as we are obedient to move as He directs—be that in worship, prayer, or prophetic declaration—God moves with power. As He shifts the spiritual atmosphere, people are drawn to Him like moths to a flame.

It is my prayer that David's tabernacle would be completely established on the earth and God's presence would invade every aspect of society. We must prepare a dwelling place for Him. It is time for our hearts to open, for us to set aside our worldly distractions—to forget about our "bowls of stew" and allow our very bodies to become His holy tabernacle. Let it be, Lord, in Jesus's mighty name!

6

THE WILDNESS OF GOD

The Holy Spirit is not the God we have created in the Western expression of Christianity. He is far more wild and wonderful. He is a consuming fire that cannot be contained (see, for example, Exodus 24:17) and He wants to reveal Himself to His people—more than we desire Him to be revealed. And believe me, when He does reveal Himself, it's something you don't want to miss.

In this chapter, I want to share a few of my favorite Holy Spirit encounters. It is my desire that these stories will increase your faith. May you believe God to experience more of who He is and may you invite Him to unleash His wild, wonderful fire in your life.

COME, HOLY SPIRIT

Toward the end of 1991, I got a call from Greg Mira, who was my pastor at that time. He was putting a worship team together for a conference in Singapore in January and he invited me to be on it. He then told me that after a discussion with the other organizers, it had been decided that I should teach a workshop.

My response was less than enthusiastic. At that time, I had only just begun to speak publicly. I also had little time to prepare. It was the end of a semester at the University of Missouri–Kansas

City Conservatory of Music, where I was a vocal performance student, and I was preparing for finals and juries—an exam performance for the vocal faculty constituting half of your grade for the semester. So it was a relatively stressful time.

"Greg," I said, "I will sing all you want me to, but I don't teach."

"Well," he said, "the Lord wants to stretch you."

When I mentioned my trepidation about the workshop to my friend Chris Hamby, he told me not to worry because he'd write something out for me and all I'd have to do was read it.

I finished the semester and spent Christmas break pretty stressed out about the upcoming conference. As the first of January arrived and it was time to leave for Singapore, I had graduated to terrified. I had sung many times, but speaking was different. This may surprise some people, but I am actually quite shy. Knowing my talk was already written for me only slightly eased my mind.

After the flight took off, I went to find Greg's seat to tell him I couldn't do it. I was just too afraid to speak in front of people. He said, "André, just have the people stand up, ask the Holy Spirit to come, and see what happens."

I remember thinking, *Well, I guess I can do that.*

In Singapore, I found out my workshop audience was the largest of the conference, with about two hundred people signed up. I said, "Lord, what are You doing? Are You trying to kill me?"

Because of my fear, Greg asked my friend Randy Wright to come along and help me out. Randy, who has since gone home to be with Jesus, was an incredible keyboard player, songwriter, and worship leader. Whenever he played, the Lord's presence came. I love imagining him now doing what he lived for, worshipping the Creator full-time in heaven.

I was still terrified when I stood up to speak, but almost instantly, the anointing came and my fear simply left. I became bold as a lion and rushed through the teaching Chris had prepared for me.

"Just sing the way God wants you to sing," I told them. Then, remembering Greg's advice, I said, "Let's stand up now and ask the Holy Spirit to come. Let's see what happens."

Randy began to play the song, "Salvation Belongs to Our God." I began to sing and as I did, the Lord's presence fell in the room like a blanket. People who had never before experienced Him in that way began to weep and fall to the floor.

The power of the Lord began setting certain people free from demonic strongholds. Others experienced emotional healing. Some received a prayer language, while others began to release prophetic words. Blown away by His faithfulness, I just stood up front and watched. I didn't have to do anything except allow God to be God, which is what I've basically done ever since.

THE CLOUD VISITS YOUNG DONG

I get to minister in South Korea quite often and I really love the Korean people. Koreans are forerunners in the 24/7 prayer movement among the nations of the earth. They have had pockets of 24/7 prayer for years. I'm guessing most people have never experienced a Korean prayer meeting, so let me just tell you that these people know how to touch heaven with their intercession and worship. Their hunger for God is infectious and their devotion to Him is humbling.

In August 1998, I went with Scott Brenner to Young Dong First Church in Seoul to do a worship conference. Young Dong is a thriving church with over-the-top hunger and passion for God. This particular time, I was teaching on prophetic worship and I began reading the account of the dedication of Solomon's temple from 2 Chronicles. As I got to the part about the cloud of God's presence filling the temple and the priests not being able to stand any longer, a cloud began coming through the back wall of the church and filling the back part of the room.

I said to the Lord, "Wow. What do You want me to do with that?"

"Stand the people up," He said.

"Okay," I replied.

At that moment, the pastor of the church, Pastor Kim, came into the meeting. As she entered, her feet literally came off of the floor and she flew backwards into the glass door. I remember thinking, *I'm sure glad the door didn't break!* Next, a woman hit the floor and began to roll from one side of the church to the other. Early Pentecostals were called "holy rollers" for this very reason.

The Lord told me to ask the people in the front to stand up and turn around to see if they could see the cloud. I turned to my interpreter, who was on the stage with me, and asked her to ask them this. As she was speaking, her eyes were opened and she could see it. A moment later, everyone in the room saw the cloud.

An angel came and stood beside me. I couldn't see him, but I knew it was an angel of His presence because I could feel fire. I asked my translator, "Can you feel the angel?" She was instantly shot backwards, making a U-turn toward the edge of the stage. I had to catch her to keep her from flying off.

The angel began to whisper in my ear. He pointed out a young man in the audience and said, "I want you to stand him up and tell him the words I am going to give to you." As the angel dictated the information, I began to prophesy this young man's destiny. Under the power of God, he hit the floor with no catcher behind him. This was around noon and he lay prostrate under the power of God until nine o'clock that evening.

We interviewed him afterward to see what the Lord had been doing. He said wave after wave of the Lord's presence had touched him. Toward the end, he'd had to use the restroom so badly, he finally asked the Lord to lift off of him so he could go and relieve himself. Apparently, God even cares about that. After nine life-changing hours, He lifted His presence so the young man could go to the restroom.

THE BUDDHIST AND THE DEER IN THE HEADLIGHTS

Another of my favorite encounters from South Korea took place many years later in April 2007. I was scheduled to minister in Young Dong as well as another church whose pastor had come to the last meeting at Young Dong. The two churches were about as different from one another as they could possibly be. Young Dong was a 24/7 house of prayer; at the other church, some members sold real estate during the week and trained for missions on weekends.

The conference at Young Dong in 1998 been full of life, wild, and off the charts. God moved with such power that at times, it seemed like a bomb had exploded, with bodies all over the floor. The other pastor had never experienced anything like it and according to Pastor Kim of Young Dong, he was nervous about what he had seen. She said he still wanted me to come to his church when I returned in 2007. Even so, he was afraid.

My colleague Eli and I met the pastor for dinner. Through his interpreter, he said they had heard about and studied the Holy Spirit, but had never really experienced Him. That explained his hesitation. People who get caught up in the business of church, while well meaning, can sometimes ignore or even shut down the more powerful movement of God. I had a feeling this pastor and his congregation were in for quite a display.

We went straight to the church from dinner. When we arrived, there were about two hundred people there worshipping. When it was time for me to speak, I said a few words and then did the only

I stopped trying to figure out

why God does what He does

a long time ago.

thing I really know how to do. I stood the people up and asked the Holy Spirit to come.

Three quarters of the room hit the floor screaming while the rest looked on, terrified like deer in the headlights. However, there was one little lady who began to run around the room, apparently ecstatic about what was going on, even though it wasn't happening to her.

I shared more about the Holy Spirit and how He moves. For the altar call, the Lord told me to call up people who had not yet received their prayer language because He wanted to give it to them. About fifty people came up front to receive, including the lady who had been so excited. Everyone received their prayer language except for her. She kept saying, "I'm so sorry." I told her she didn't have to be sorry and assured her she would eventually receive it.

After the meeting, I learned she was a Buddhist, which explained why she didn't receive a prayer language, a gift from God reserved for believers in Jesus. I couldn't stop thinking about her—and it still gets to me. I wrote earlier about the world being hungry for the supernatural. What's more supernatural than the power of God? This lady wasn't even a believer, yet was deliriously excited about seeing God's awesome power. It's as if she was saying, "I don't really understand this, but I want it."

Meanwhile, a good number of the Christians—who should have been desirous to see God move in even *greater* power—were afraid. An actual encounter with the Almighty was almost too much for these business-focused believers…but only almost. That nervous pastor must have seen or felt something he liked because we were invited back the following night.

ENTERTAINING ANGELS

Not all the awesome stories come from Asia. In the late nineties, RAIN ministries, the Resurrection Apostolic International

Network based out of the Twin Cities area of Minnesota, established something called City Church. Every Friday night, different churches met together to seek the Lord.

One particular night, I'd been asked to speak. As I was sharing, the Lord began to move in the room. I responded as I usually do. I stopped, asked the people to stand, and invited the Holy Spirit to come. He manifested with waves of His glory.

A young lady who kind of looked like a "biker chick" fell to the floor and called for me to come over to her. She said, "André, I'm stuck to the floor and I can't get up."

I said, "It's okay—there is just a big angel sitting on you."

This seemed to calm her down, so I continued with the meeting. Later that night, she testified she had always asked God for a big biker angel to be with her! She said while she was on the floor, she'd asked the Lord why she couldn't get up and He'd asked her if she remembered praying for the big biker angel. She did, she'd told Him. The Lord had said, "I answered your prayer. He's sitting on you right now."

You may be wondering what a big biker angel is or why he would sit on someone. Honestly, I don't have a clue. Maybe the only explanation is "because he can." I stopped trying to figure out why God does what He does a long time ago. He is God and I am not. His thoughts are not mine (see Isaiah 55:8) and what seems to be foolishness to me is wisdom to Him (see 1 Corinthians 1:25.) So if He wanted to send this lady a biker angel, I say, "Great!"

A couple of young boys, about five and six years old, were also at the meeting that night. The Lord began to move on them, so I called them up to pray over them. When I did, they fell to the floor and lay there for a while. Suddenly, they got up, and began to point out people and give them powerful prophetic words. Then they fell down again for a while and the process began all over again. This went on for quite some time.

Later, they explained that they were having encounters with angels while they were out on the floor. The angels would minister to them, tell them who to give a word to, and tell them exactly what to say. When they got up, they would just do what the angels had told them to do.

When God comes, He brings His royal entourage with Him. There was a lot of angelic activity that night. We worship Jesus, not angels, but I am always glad when they show up.

SUPERNATURAL WEIGHT LOSS

Another time, while I was living in Minnesota, the Lord woke me up in the middle of the night to tell me what He wanted me to do in a meeting the next day. (See, for example, John 16:13.) This was unusual for me. Typically, the moment I get up to minister is when the Lord gives me direction for the meeting.

That night, the Lord told me to have the women stand up and break the spirit of misogyny off them. Misogyny is an ingrained prejudice or dislike of women, and the Lord said He wanted me, as a man, to represent men and repent for putting false expectations of beauty on them and trying to hold them back from His purposes in their lives. He told me two things were going to happen: some women would begin to go through deliverance and some would have supernatural weight loss.

The next day, I did as the Lord had asked. I invited the women to stand up. When I began the act of identification repentance, about a hundred of them fell to the floor screaming. The Holy Spirit began delivering them from things that had bound them for years.

Afterward, some of the ladies came up to show me that they had instantly lost weight. One lady came literally holding up her pants. God is concerned about every intimate detail of our lives.

He cared about the trauma those women had experienced and He came to set them free.

BREAKING THE WITCH DOCTOR'S CURSE

Here's another wonderful story of deliverance from the power of evil. I was in Alaska for the Healing Rooms of Alaska conference. After worship, as I got up to minister, I noticed the room was packed with people. All of the pastors were sitting up front, wearing nice suits. In my jeans and shirt, I felt kind of out of place.

Then, as I began to minister, the power of the Lord fell. People began to scream and run around; the sound was deafening. One lady jumped up and began to dance wildly around the room. When she got up front, she fell prostrate on top of one of the seated pastors. He stared at me, shocked, with a look that clearly said, "What is going on here?" I remember thinking, *This shouldn't be weird to them. They're Pentecostals.*

Later, I found out that the dancing woman was a missionary on a First Nations' reservation. A witch doctor had come to her home to put a curse on her and after he left, she'd become deathly ill. She had visited many doctors, but could not get any relief. For a long time, she'd had no energy or strength to do anything, let alone dance with enthusiasm around a room.

The power of God broke the power of the curse and she was set free that night. God healed her body and she went back to the reservation to faithfully serve Him. She remained there for years until the Lord finally took her home to be with Him.

GOLD FALLING FROM HEAVEN

One of my favorite encounters occurred at Christ Bible Discipleship Worship Center in Marshville, North Carolina, because of the way the fire of the Holy Spirit spread. I was there for a two-day meeting and the first night was a struggle. There was a lot of spiritual warfare from the enemy, so there was not much breakthrough that evening.

Back at the hotel later, I repented of everything I could think of. The next morning, I spent two hours with the Lord just seeking His presence. When we walked into the church that second night, we could tell immediately that the atmosphere was different. The Lord began to move with power. All around, people were being touched by the presence of God. Manifestations of the Holy Spirit, like gold dust and even feathers, began to appear.

They still fall at this congregation to this day. The streets in heaven are made of gold so when we pray for God's kingdom to come on earth as it is in heaven, maybe that's why something like this occurs!

That night, the Lord told me He was going to give people gold fillings and even gold teeth—and sure enough, thirteen people testified to finding gold teeth in their mouths that night, including the pastor's mother, who went to her dentist the next day to verify what had happened. She asked him what he had put in her mouth and he told her that her fillings were silver amalgam. "Not anymore," she said. The dentist examined her mouth and discovered that not only were her fillings no longer silver, but her teeth had turned to solid gold.

The pastor's mother went to visit family in Florida, eager to show everyone what God had done for her. They were all excited and wanted to see the gold teeth—all except for her nephew's girlfriend, a pastor's daughter who had been wounded by the church. She had no desire to see gold teeth, nor was she interested in hearing about them. But the next morning as she brushed her hair, something like gold dust began to fall from it. That supernatural manifestation of the glory of God in the form of gold dust radically changed her life and she is once again walking with God.

Still others were touched by this miracle of gold falling from heaven to earth, even though they were not present that night. One of the pastor's right-hand men had fallen away from God and was at home during the two nights of meetings. At the same time the Lord released the wonderful display of gold at the church, the man was covered with gold dust—in his home.

The next day, when he heard what had happened at the church, he returned and gave his heart completely to the Lord. An encounter with God is powerful indeed!

"MAKE SOMEONE FLY"

For five years, I was the main speaker at a youth camp in the mountains outside of Seattle. God did many amazing things there, like filling the room with the glory cloud and opening all the kids' eyes to see it, and causing gold dust to appear on the kids, especially those who didn't believe it could happen to them. One guy insisted it was all a bunch of hooey—until he put his hands in his pockets and pulled them out covered in gold dust.

Parents sent their kids to the camp hoping they would get a touch from God. Most of them were pretty hard cases, very rebellious. But God loves the hard cases—and nothing is too hard for Him.

I remember one young man who came up front proclaiming he was an atheist. He decided to give God a test and said, "God, if You're real, make someone fly."

What do you think happened next? The presence of the Lord came with force and kids became so filled with the Holy Spirit that they acted like the people in Acts 2:13–17. Suddenly, one of the kids began to fly—literally. His feet lifted off the floor, he flew out the door, and he landed in the snow across the parking lot. Needless to say, the young man who put the challenge before God is no longer an atheist.

I hope these stories have done for you what they did for me. My encounters with the power of His presence have ruined me for normal church. I'm forever asking God to show me even greater manifestations. I hope you will join me in that prayer. Remember, Jesus said, *"Whoever believes in me will do the works I have been doing, and they will do even greater things than these"* (John 14:12 NIV).

7

THE HUDSON VALLEY REVIVAL

Seeing the Holy Spirit move in a meeting is glorious and wonderful, but it's even better when you get to see a move of God unfold in a particular city or region over a period of weeks, months, and even years. This is when you really get to witness the spiritual shifts that lead to lasting transformation in individuals, families, and communities.

In 2003, I had the privilege of taking part in such a move of God in upstate New York. After meeting Phil and Paige Todd while ministering at Gateway Fellowship in West Haven, Connecticut, they asked me to come and minister for a few days at their church, Glory Oasis Church in the Hudson Valley, which I agreed to do.

At the time, I had temporarily become very disillusioned with ministry and was trying to find a secular job. Even though I didn't want to go and minister in the Hudson Valley, I decided I would. I had already said yes and I wanted to be a man of my word. But I promised myself that as soon I got back to Minneapolis, I was getting a regular job. A friend of mine was an executive at Macy's and had set up an interview for me there. I was looking forward to it.

Glory Oasis was a small church that, unbeknownst to me, had only started in January of that year. Though they were small and young, this group was hungry for the presence of the Lord and were contending for an historic move of God. The pastor, Angella Reid, was a former Wall Street executive who had attended the early meetings of pastor and evangelist Rodney Howard-Browne in upstate New York. During that time, God had called her out of secular employment and led her into ministry. Because of what she had experienced in the presence of the Lord, she was not satisfied with ordinary church. For ten months, she and her small congregation had been seeking more. I arrived in the Hudson Valley on Friday, October 24, 2003. Matthew Ferrell, a worship leader from Seattle, Washington, had agreed to join me at Glory Oasis and teach a two-and-a-half-day worship seminar. Matt led worship that night and it was explosive right from the start. I remember thinking, *These folks know how to worship!* God came with such power that I was blown away. Even though I had sung prophetically on worship teams for years, I had never seen God come with such intensity during worship.

When I got up to minister, I prophesied for an hour and a half, relaying detailed information about the region—things I could not have known. This was also new to me. It was as if the Holy Spirit took possession of my voice. I had no control over it. God revealed history about the region going back about a hundred and fifty years. He said He was releasing an anointing of the Quakers of church history again in that area. He had a covenant with the land and because of the promises made to the forefathers, He was releasing His power.

Then I saw an angel digging in the ground so fast, his arms were a blur. I asked the Lord what he was doing and the Lord told me the angel was re-digging the nineteenth-century evangelist Charles Finney's well of revival. I had no idea Charles Finney had previously ministered in the area.

God moved powerfully that night; there were bodies all over the floor. The pastor asked me if I would pray about extending the meetings so the movement of God could continue. I did the religious thing and said, "Yes, of course I will pray," but in my heart I was thinking, *I am going to finish my commitment on Sunday morning, go home, and get a regular job.*

STEPPING OVER THE LINE

The next day, we started the meeting at about ten in the morning. Matthew taught on Revelation 5:8 for about forty-five minutes and then the Lord took over. His power and presence began to fall on people. As one person would repent, another would worship, and still another would begin to prophesy. Several strong prophetic words came out from the people that day. One was that we had a *kairos*, a divinely appointed moment, where we could call back to the Lord those we loved who had walked away from Him, especially those the Lord said had a major call on their lives.

At about three in the afternoon, while all of this was going on at the church, the Lord fell on Eli, the young man I mentioned in the last chapter who later became my colleague. He'd been out all night partying and was at home sleeping off a hangover. He said he woke up and heard the phone downstairs ring three different times. He knew the first call came from his friends, inviting him to party, and the second was from his brother with the same invitation. He didn't answer those calls. He was finally tired of that lifestyle. He had tried to get out of it before and had even checked himself into rehab, but just couldn't get free from the bondage.

The third phone call, he knew, came from his mother. He also knew she was calling because she wanted him to come to church. He jumped out of the bed and ran downstairs to answer the phone. He agreed to go to church to appease his mother, who had promised to buy him dinner. He said he figured he would just humor her and go to church—at least he would get some dinner and feel better.

Sometimes when you are in your most physical mindset, God releases some of His greatest gifts.

Eli had given his heart to the Lord previously and tried the whole church thing, but it had never seemed to work for him. Still, there was an excitement building in him. He knew something was different. He found himself eager for his mother to come and take him to church.

When he arrived at church, he later told me, it was as if the oppression on him couldn't come through the door with him. Eli said everything became brighter and he could see his life clearly. He felt the presence of God and began to pace in the back of the room. Soon, Phil Todd noticed him and went to talk to him.

As soon as I saw Eli, the Lord began to download information to me about his life. I called him forward and prophesied over him. He said he had never experienced anything like that before. It was exciting, but he needed more of God. If that was all there was, what was the point?

He asked me for the microphone, so I gave it to him. He said he needed God and he believed we knew Him. But, he asked, if he couldn't have access to God because of the way he looked and lived, what was he to do? All over the room, people began to weep and rush forward, hugging him and committing to pray for him and be there for him.

Phil drew an imaginary line in the sand. He told Eli that one side was the life he was living and the other side was the new life God was offering. Phil asked him if he was really ready to enter into a new life with Jesus. Eli thought about it for a second or two, then happily jumped across the line.

More than ten years later, Eli is still living that new life. He's traveled all over the world with me as my assistant. The Lord has used Eli to teach me about His love and grace. He will never give up on us. He is faithful.

AN IMPOSSIBLE TASK

After the meeting, I called my friend William Ford to tell him what was going on. "Will, I am touching something I have never touched before." I told him about Eli, and Will said he was a prophetic picture of Isaiah 22:22. He also explained that Eli is short for Eliachim, which means "set up by God" in Hebrew and has the connotation of awakening from a stupor. I said, "Will, did I tell you he had been asleep with a hangover?"

Saturday's meeting lasted a full ten hours. God was simply unstoppable. Angella came to me again that night and said, "We need to continue." I agreed to do one more meeting on Sunday night. I still wanted to just go home and get a regular job, so without telling anyone, I put what I thought was an impossible task before God, praying, "Lord, if You want me to stay and continue with these meetings, tomorrow night—with no advertisement— let there be standing room only when the meetings start."

Mind you, there had only been around forty people there the whole weekend. I figured I'd be back in Minneapolis and working at Macy's in no time. But sometimes when you are in your most physical mindset, God releases some of His greatest gifts. As you might have guessed, when I walked into the church Sunday night, there was standing room only. You would think I would have been excited, but actually, I just got mad. I had to go outside to get my heart right before the Lord. Thank God for grace.

After Sunday's meeting, I called my friend Scott Brenner to tell him what was happening. He said, "André, that sounds like the Welsh Revival." He read me an email he had just received about that revival in the early 1900s, where God moved powerfully on the people. I learned that Evan Roberts, the young man God used to spark that revival, basically just stewarded the meetings. He rarely preached. That was exactly what had happened that weekend in the Hudson Valley. I told Scott I had been in Wales in May and had stood in the very spot where Evan Roberts had preached.

Not only that, I told him, but while I was there, the curator of Moriah Chapel told me that though most people believe the Holy Spirit fell on October 31, He actually fell on the twenty-fifth while the young people met together to pray. On October 25, almost one hundred years later, we had the ten-hour meeting. Scott said I must have brought something back.

HEAVEN AND NATURE SING

Even the heavens marked what happened in the Hudson Valley that weekend. Remarkable solar activity was recorded the day we began the meetings. A lady named Pam told me she had dreamed a year earlier that when revival came to the Northeast, there would be signs in the heavens. On Thursday, October 30, the Northern Lights came over the Hudson Valley in bright red mixed with blue and white. From what I understand, the Northern Lights hadn't appeared in the area for about forty years.

That night, people described something very unusual—they began to dance with angels. One lady danced for an hour—around bodies on the floor as well as instruments and furniture—with her eyes completely closed and never touched a thing. She would get close to running into things and I would become concerned, but she would always turn and go in another direction just in time. Impossible—unless you are being led by an angel of God!

Also, the last time the Hudson Valley had received the amount of rain it got that October was when evangelist Rodney Howard-Browne's ministry was birthed there. Israel, too, received an incredible amount of rainfall both times: during the beginning of Howard-Browne's ministry and then again during this new season of revival.

HEALING AND DELIVERANCE

The testimonies of changed lives in this move of God were amazing. One lady, whose two brothers were killed by the same man about twenty years before, came to the realization that she had not forgiven the killer. The Lord revealed to her there was a pocket of pus in her heart, marking her desire for revenge. He told her to publicly repent and pray for this man, which she did. With tears streaming down her face, she forgave and prayed for the man who had killed her brothers and God completely healed her heart of bitterness.

Others with longstanding unforgiveness issues called and asked to be forgiven by the people with whom they had the issues. An incredible amount of restoration occurred. People began to really love each other. Love is a miracle. In fact, receiving and giving love is one of the greatest miracles of all.

One lady said she went to the meetings that weekend because the Lord told her to go. She had not been in church for four years and had not heard from anyone about what was going on at Glory Oasis. But God told her there was a move happening there and she needed to be present. He told her He was going to heal her heart.

A gentleman who was raised Catholic said the Lord came and stood before him. He saw and felt Him reach inside him and pull something out. He said he could feel something being ripped out of him—from his toes to his head. As he hit the floor, the Lord said He was delivering him from a spirit of religion. Isn't it amazing how personal and real God is?

A lady who was on oxygen 24/7 and taking one hundred different types of medication came and fell under the power of His presence. She lay on the floor under the power of the Holy Spirit for hours. When she got up, she left the meeting pushing the oxygen container, no longer needing it. Her doctor lowered the number of her medications from one hundred types to only five. Our God is an awesome God!

THE FIRE SPREADS

On Sunday night, a lady who was a minister came to the meeting. She said when she walked in the room, she heard what sounded like pipes bursting. She turned around and saw the throne of God coming into the room. She fell prostrate to the floor and remained there the rest of the night. The next day, she got on an airplane and flew out to minister at a conference that was conservative in nature. Her instructions had been to bring a brown suit and a blue suit and let them handle everything else. When she got up to speak, she raised her hands. All over the room, people began to fall under the power of God as the Lord moved in the same way He was moving back in the Hudson Valley.

Additionally, while Matt Ferrell was ministering with me in New York that Sunday morning, the Lord moved with power back in Seattle, Washington, at his home church. The worship leader there who was substituting for Matt suddenly shot backwards and hit the wall as God did in Washington what He was doing in New York.

Needless to say, we continued the meetings, but unfortunately, Matt had to fly home so he could get back to his part-time job. He had taken the job because his church couldn't afford to pay him a full-time salary to direct the house of prayer and be the worship pastor. Matt hated going back to the part-time job. He said he could feel the demonic oppression there constantly. Reluctantly, he boarded a plane home, only to experience the Lord falling upon him during the flight. He began to weep and couldn't seem to stop. The Lord also came upon the girl seated next to him, so Matt got to minister to her. Simultaneously, God was bringing repentance at our meetings in New York like I have never experienced before or since. People all over the room began to weep, crying out their sins.

The next morning, Matt went to the job he hated, still crying and shaking under the power of God. His manager asked him what was going on. When he told her, she became open to the gospel of Jesus Christ, which she never had been before. According to Matt, the atmosphere changed completely. The demons that had ruled the place could no longer be felt.

As you can see, what happened at Glory Oasis wasn't contained in those four walls. It began to spread, especially throughout the Hudson Valley.

Joey, a stylist at an upscale hair salon in Westchester County, New York, had been at the meetings. He said when he went back to work, he couldn't stop jerking and reacting to the power and the presence of the Holy Spirit while trying to cut the hair of his mostly Jewish clientele. Interestingly, woman after woman suddenly wanted to talk about Jesus. One client sat down in his chair and just began to weep. When he asked her what was wrong, she said, "I don't know. There is just something in this shop." Well, we know the "something" was the presence of the Lord.

Another lady who was a minister came on Friday night, then returned home to minister at her church on Sunday morning. When she got up to speak, the Lord fell and began to touch people all over the room with His power.

Two co-pastors of a local congregation also attended meetings that week. When they opened the service at their church on Sunday morning at ten, God broke out. When they looked at the clock again, it was 4:30 p.m. No one had preached a sermon.

FREEING THE CHILDREN

Children were also touched by the power of God. One night, everyone under the age of twenty got his or her prayer language. God gripped the hearts of young people in rebellion with His love. Many of them were unable to stand. Some wrestled on the floor with angels for hours.

One couple was particularly desperate for God to move. Their son was horribly demonized, so they brought him with them for prayer. However, they couldn't get him out of the car; he refused to come into the church. The parents came in for a while, but because they were from a somewhat conservative background, what was happening was too much for them and they left. Unbeknownst to them, they had received an impartation of the presence of God in the short period of time they were there.

The next day, back at the feed store they owned, the son began to manifest his demon. Yet this time, something was different. The power of the Lord rose up in the mother. She pointed at her son and rebuked the demon. Right in the middle of the store, the boy began to throw up and was completely delivered. Praise the Lord!

SO MUCH FOR MACY'S

The meetings continued every night for about six weeks. After that, they ran Wednesday through Sunday nights for about six months. I relocated from Minneapolis to be a part of what God was doing there, while still maintaining my itinerant ministry schedule. So much for Macy's.

I brought in many of my ministry friends to sow into what God was doing and they always left a deposit of His grace. Dr. Brian Simmons, author of *The Passion Translation* of the Bible, came and saw what looked like a waterfall in the back of the room. He said, "André, this feels like the Toronto Blessing." (That was

God's presence was so tangible,
there were lightning-like flashes in
the church.

a sustained move of God that broke out in Toronto, Canada, in January 1994, but possibly with more angelic activity.)

So many things happened during this period that, again, it utterly ruined me for normal church life. God's presence was so tangible, there were lightning-like flashes of light in the church. The wind once blew so hard we could feel it and hear it in the room. I asked a man to make sure the furnace wasn't on and he said the furnace was off. It was the wind of the Spirit.

I believe that wind is about to blow again. The Hudson Valley revival was just a taste of what God is going to do when He unleashes greater dimensions of His glory. He is about to step in like "a rushing mighty wind" (Acts 2:2) and release His presence—not just in one localized place, but in entire regions. Everything is about to shift and He has invited us to participate with Him. This is the greatest time to be alive on the earth. Just think: He could have chosen Moses, Paul, or any other of the patriarchs of the faith to be part of this work, but He picked us. He picked now. So get ready!

8

LIVING WITH THE SPIRIT

Now that you've read about how God's presence comes, how lives are transformed, and you have become wrecked for "business as usual" for the rest of your days, let's take a look at what a life and a church led by the Spirit looks like. What does it mean when the Lord decides to bless us in this way?

God once told me, "André, when I say I am going to bless you, you think it means I am going to give you stuff. You think I'm going to give you a better car or a better house. If that were the case, then I am blessing a lot of drug dealers and I am blessing a lot of Hollywood actors who profane My name. When I say I am going to bless you, I mean I am going to give you Myself. My blessing is My presence."

It is from His presence that we receive everything we need, so if we need a better house or more money, we become eligible for those blessings by allowing His presence to permeate our lives. In order to be blessed, we need to be presence-driven people, led by the Holy Spirit.

People ask me, "André, what is your five-year plan?" I always say something like, "I don't know. I'm just trying to get through today." I don't know what my five-year plan is. I'm not good with all that stuff; that is just not who I am. I want to be led by the Holy

The Holy Spirit is continually releasing His creative, resurrection power in our lives.

Spirit and the endearing presence of the Lord. I want to go where He says to go and I want to stop only when and where He says to stop.

HE IS THE GIFT

The presence of God is His Spirit. Let's take a moment to consider just a few aspects of who the Holy Spirit is to us and what an overwhelming blessing this greatest gift is in our lives.

First, the Holy Spirit is our teacher, leader, and liberator. Jesus said:

> "When he, the Spirit of truth, comes, he will guide you into all the truth. He will not speak on his own; he will speak only what he hears, and he will tell you what is yet to come. He will glorify me because it is from me that he will receive what he will make known to you."   (John 16:13–14 NIV)

The Spirit leads us into truth and His truth sets us free.

Next, the Holy Spirit is our helper, the *paracletos*, "one who is called alongside." We may say to ourselves, "Oh, isn't that nice? The Holy Spirit is called alongside us to help. He's the nice little helper." In reality, if you look to the Greek, it goes much deeper than that. Some theologians describe it this way: When the enemy comes against you, the Holy Spirit comes against the enemy—with a vengeance. Others refer to it as the "insanity" of the Holy Spirit. He goes crazy against whatever is attacking you. Isaiah 59:19 says, "*When the enemy comes in like a flood, the Spirit of the* LORD *will lift up a standard against him.*" I like to read it this way: "When the enemy comes in, **like a flood** the Spirit of the Lord will lift up a standard against him."

The Holy Spirit, like Jesus, is also our comforter and our intercessor. Romans 8:26 declares the Spirit prays for us with *"groanings"* and utterances too deep for words. When you are going through something that's really deep, sometimes there are no words. All you can do is groan. Now imagine the Holy Spirit, He who prays for you and makes intercession for you. He is so utterly on your side that there are no words for Him either. He just begins to groan and as He groans, the Father understands. When we hurt so deeply that we can't understand—or be understood—the Spirit, our intercessor, *can* be understood by the Father.

CREATIVITY RELEASED

Again, the Holy Spirit is in our lives as the liberator, leader, teacher, protector, intercessor, and defender for one purpose: to help us grow up into mature sons and daughters who fully reflect the Son of God, Jesus. He is continually releasing His creative, resurrection power in our lives for this purpose.

There is a theological concept called the "law of first mention." When God sets a precedent in Scripture, that's the way He's going to do it all the way through. I was on the platform in Korea once when the Lord said to me, "André, I never really change My mind."

I said, "Okay, what do You mean?"

He replied, "When I start out in a certain way, I continue in that way. I never really change the way I do things. If you open up the Bible, in Genesis 1, what does it say? It says, 'The Spirit of the Lord hovered over the face of the deep.' Then, out of that, creativity began to happen."

Applying the law of first mention, what the Lord was saying to me was, "This is the way I do it. I release My presence—I release My Spirit. You are led by the Spirit and out of My Spirit comes creativity."

Paul wrote we have this treasure—the creative Spirit of God—in us as *"earthen vessels"* or *"jars of clay"* (NIV):

For it is the God who commanded light to shine out of darkness, who has shone in our hearts to give the light of the knowledge of the glory of God in the face of Jesus Christ. But we have this treasure in earthen vessels, that the excellence of the power may be of God and not of us.   (2 Corinthians 4:6–7)

The Spirit in us is the same God who said, *"Let there be light"* (Genesis 1:3), and the light shone out of darkness. This is the same God whose Spirit hovered over the face of the deep. He mentioned that for a reason. The Lord doesn't just do things because He has nothing else to say. He was trying to release a specific thing by saying the Holy Spirit was hovering over the face of the deep. Out of that place in His presence, that place of His hovering, creativity was released.

It's the same with us. The Holy Spirit comes and lives inside us. He hovers over us and out of that place of abiding in Him, of being led by God's Spirit, creativity is released and we move into the places He has for us.

CHRISTIANITY 101

The Western church is in desperate need of a mind-shift about the Holy Spirit and about the spirit realm in general. Some time, I want to take a whole group of Americans to Korea to teach them how to worship. I really do. In the United States, you have to prime the pump: "Come on, lift your hands and jump!" Over there, you just strum the guitar or play the piano and they're right there. It doesn't matter whether the person can sing. It doesn't matter if they hit a clunker. None of that really matters. People just go into that place of worship. In the East, people already understand there's more to God and they want to experience it.

In Korea, I had another interesting conversation with the Lord. There were three thousand to five thousand people in an

Olympic stadium worshipping like crazy with all their heart, soul, and strength. I was thinking, *God, this is amazing!*

The Lord said, "André, you've been taught that I move in third-world nations because they are more desperate, because they can't get to doctors and that kind of thing. Some of that is true, but the reality is this: those people have an awareness of the supernatural. They understand there is something greater than themselves and when I reveal to them that *I am* that 'something greater,' they have an expectation that I will move in power."

He went on, "In America, in the West, you have three problems. First, you have to get people to believe there is something greater than themselves because, second, humanism has captured the West. The third problem is getting them to agree that it's Me who is greater."

Let me give you an illustration of the difference in expectation that the Lord pointed out to me. After people in the West read about a great revival that broke out in Indonesia, they traveled there to investigate reports of people walking on water, raising the dead, and experiencing other miraculous events. These pilgrims arrived in Indonesia and said, "We hear some incredible things are happening here."

But the Indonesians responded, "Well, not really—nothing out of the ordinary."

The people from the West were upset, saying, "But wait a minute. We were told—we read in the book—that folks were walking on water and raising the dead."

The Indonesians responded, "Well, yes, but that's all in the Bible. That's Christianity 101."

You can see the issue—it's a difference of mindset. We get a little taste of God and we go, "That was great. Thanks, God. You can go back to heaven now. I can handle things from here." Instead, we must allow ourselves to be saturated by His presence,

His Spirit, His anointing. Let's become drenched in the supernatural works of Jesus so we keep saying, "We want to see more." Then, and only then, can we begin to step into His greater works.

SATURATED WITH HIS PRESENCE

Do you want to know how to live a holy life? Get in the presence of the Lord! King David wrote, *"You will show me the path of life; in Your presence is fullness of joy; at Your right hand are pleasures forevermore"* (Psalm 16:11).

Why do we try to live apart from the presence of God? Why do we try to live like we can do it on our own?

Sometimes, American ingenuity is a good thing. Pull yourself up by your bootstraps—you can make it. Other times, it is a curse. Our nation does not have the dependency on God that we desperately need. Think of the awful events of September 11, 2001. For a while, we turned back to God as a nation. Then we said, "We're America. We can beat anyone. We will do it."

We must understand that we need the presence of God. We have to be led by the Spirit. Ephesians 5:18 says, *"And do not be drunk with wine...but be filled with the Spirit."* We need to be saturated to overflowing. Of course, when you are filled with the Holy Spirit, you may appear to be drunk, as the disciples seemed to be on the day of Pentecost. But who cares what it looks like? Who cares what people say? Do you want to please man or God?

I, for one, am tired of being a man-pleaser. I want to be a God-pleaser. I want His presence to come and saturate me because in His presence, there is fullness of joy. Joy is totally different than happiness. Happiness is based on circumstances. Things are good and we are happy. When things aren't so good, we're kind of down. That's how happiness works. It's conditional. But joy, like God's love, is unconditional. Joy comes from the quiet confidence that God knows what is best for you and He is in your corner.

When you confess that God loves you, you create an atmosphere for Him to show His goodness to you.

Regardless of what you are going through, when His presence saturates you, the joy of the Lord remains with you.

A GOD ENCOUNTER WAITING TO HAPPEN

I came from a really rough background. I did not know what love was. I was abused, mistreated, and hated by my family. As I've mentioned, I am really very real with God. He truly is my Father. I remember telling the Lord, "Look, I can't say You love me just because You say You do. You have to show me."

The Lord spoke to me then, saying, "André, you need to understand one thing. When you begin to confess that I love you and I'm good to you, even when you don't see it in your present circumstances, you create an atmosphere for My love to get to you—for Me to show My goodness to you."

If we keep saying, "God, I can't see that You are good to me. I can't see that You love me," then guess what? Our experiences are going to dictate our relationship with Him. Instead, we should confess, "God, You love me. God, You are good to me. The Word of God says You are a good God, that Your mercy endures forever. The Word of God says You will never leave me nor forsake me, Lord. It says You will love me with an everlasting love." Then our experiences begin to line up with that confession.

I believe this same teaching applies to experiencing the presence of God. We begin to confess that the Word of God says He's with us, that we hear His voice, and that His presence will follow those who believe. We confess and guess what? All of a sudden, things around us begin to move. We don't have to work at it; it just begins to happen. Everywhere we walk, we become a God encounter waiting to happen.

This is what Smith Wigglesworth, the British evangelist and faith healer, meant when he said, in effect, "If the Spirit doesn't move me, I'll move Him." He had a revelation that God was inside him and that the Spirit of the Lord was with him and leading him. If the Holy Spirit was leading him, he reasoned, then everywhere he went, he was a God encounter waiting to happen. He wasn't waiting on God; God was waiting on him. God was already there.

LOOK, THE CLOUD IS MOVING

The Old Testament provides us with a powerful picture of what it is like to follow the Holy Spirit wherever He leads:

So it was always: the cloud covered it by day, and the appearance of fire by night. Whenever the cloud was taken up from above the tabernacle, after that the children of Israel would journey; and in the place where the cloud settled, there the children of Israel would pitch their tents. At the command of the Lord the children of Israel would journey, and at the command of the Lord they would camp; as long as the cloud stayed above the tabernacle they remained encamped. Even when the cloud continued long, many days above the tabernacle, the children of Israel kept the charge of the Lord and did not journey. So it was, when the cloud was above the tabernacle a few days: according to the command of the Lord they would remain encamped, and according to the command of the Lord they would journey. So it was, when the cloud remained only from evening until morning: when the cloud was taken up in the morning, then they would journey; whether by day or by night, whenever the cloud was taken up, they would journey. Whether it was two days, a month, or a year that the cloud remained above the tabernacle, the children of Israel would remain encamped and not journey; but when it was taken up, they would journey. At the command of the Lord they remained encamped, and at the command of the Lord they journeyed; they kept the charge of the Lord, at

*the command of the L*ORD *by the hand of Moses.*
(Numbers 9:16–23)

Imagine this scene. There were over a million people following a cloud, the presence of God. The cloud would either remain above the tabernacle for a period of time or it would move. The Israelites had no control over it. They would set up camp if the cloud was at rest. Each morning, as this massive crowd of people woke, if the cloud lifted and began to move, they had to pack up their belongings and tents, which they may have just set up the night before. "Well, okay, the cloud is moving," they might have said. "Time to follow the cloud."

I'm not sure many of us could handle living with this level of obedience. Many of us like tradition and we don't like change. For us, the cloud begins to move and we say, "No, I am comfortable where I am." So we stay. We hold on to our tradition.

Do you realize that every denomination was born in some form of revival? The people decided to camp around their experience and stop following the cloud. Then, when the presence of the Lord began to move in a fresh way, they said, "No, I like it here. I am going to camp. Lord, You can go on, but I am going to stay here." Baptists stayed with baptism, Methodists stayed with their method, and so on.

Those of us who have been part of what is known as the Third Wave are stuck in the particulars of the original movement. But the Lord is saying, "Look, the cloud is moving. Follow My presence. If I am only here for a day, then you camp for a day. If you want My blessing, if you want the glory you say you want, then when the cloud lifts, you go." Now, obviously, we are to keep the central doctrines of the church, such as the virgin birth, the authority of the Scriptures, and the second coming of Jesus. These never change. But we are to keep pressing in to God for a visitation of His glorious presence in each of our lives and in each generation!

The Lord will gladly make us uncomfortable where we are so He can move us to the next place. The psalmist wrote, "*The voice of the* LORD *shakes the wilderness; the* LORD *shakes the Wilderness of Kadesh*" (Psalm 29:8). *Kadesh* means "sanctuary." Sanctuary represents the things we hold on to, the place we feel safe. Sanctuary is comfort. When the voice of the Lord comes, it shakes what makes us comfortable so we can learn to depend on Him for our comfort.

We have go with the cloud. But of course, some of us don't move easily. So God does what a bird does when it's trying to teach its little ones how to fly. First, He starts pulling the comfortable things out of our nest. Life gets kind of prickly and doesn't feel as nice as it used to. If you're feeling uncomfortable, like something is poking you, that something may be the Lord, pulling the soft places out of your nest. He might let that poking become really painful, if that's what it takes to bring you to the edge. Then, before you know what's happening, He will push you over that edge. And in that terrifying, divine moment, you finally realize something: you have wings. You just have to flap them and you'll catch the wind. You begin to follow the Holy Spirit.

"SHOW ME YOUR GLORY"

In Exodus 32 and 33, Moses had just had a major encounter with God—a forty-day visitation. (I don't know about you, but I'm still waiting on a one-day visitation.) When he comes down from the mountain, Moses discovers that in his absence, the people had basically lost their minds and were partying and dancing around a golden calf.

Most of us would be tempted to say, "I quit. Okay? I'm not doing this anymore, God. I'm done." What does Moses do? He convinces God not to kill them all. He converses one-on-one with God, and God listens to him and spares the lives of His people.

Then God tells Moses it's time to move again. This time, Moses is hesitant.

Then Moses said to the LORD, "See, You say to me, 'Bring up this people.' But You have not let me know whom You will send with me. Yet You have said, 'I know you by name, and you have also found grace in My sight.' Now therefore, I pray, if I have found grace in Your sight, show me now Your way, that I may know You and that I may find grace in Your sight. And consider that this nation is Your people." And He said, "My Presence will go with you, and I will give you rest." Then he said to Him, "If Your Presence does not go with us, do not bring us up from here. For how then will it be known that Your people and I have found grace in Your sight, except You go with us? So we shall be separate, Your people and I, from all the people who are upon the face of the earth." So the LORD said to Moses, "I will also do this thing that you have spoken; for you have found grace in My sight, and I know you by name." And he said, "Please, show me Your glory."
(Exodus 33:12–18)

Remember, Moses had just had a forty-day encounter with God. This man, who already knew more of God than any other man on the earth, was saying, "I have to see Your face. I have to know You are with me. I have to be led by Your presence. I talked to You and that was cool. I saw You on the mountain. I've seen You come down in fire. But, God, that isn't enough. I want to see Your face."

God is so big, so vast, so incredible. Yet many of us take a little sliver and say, "Thanks, I'm satisfied. I've had enough." But Moses, who had experienced far, far more, said, "Lord, there's got to be more. Lord, show me Your face." Moses was desperate for more. I believe God wants to release that same spirit of longing into His body today. He wants to release a desperate cry in us, where we've

God is willing to do anything to make us desperate for the blessing of the Spirit.

seen a lot, but we are not satisfied. He wants us to exclaim, "There's got to be more than this! Show me Your glory. I want to see Your face. I have to know You're with me. Release Your glory to me now. I want to be led by the fire by night and the cloud by day. I'm not going to settle for anything less than that. I have to be led by Your presence. God, until I know You are with me, I'm not moving from this place!"

How many of us in the church are truly desperate like that? How many will say we're not going to settle for second-class, status-quo Christianity anymore? Are we ready to say we will no longer be apathetic Christians who just skate into heaven without experiencing the presence of God while we are still on earth? He does not want us to be satisfied with walking around and saying, "I'm good—I got my ticket to heaven." He wants us to know the fire and the presence of the living God like never before. We have to be led by His Spirit.

WHAT IS YOUR NAME?

God is willing to do anything to make us as desperate for the blessing of the Spirit as Jacob was when he wrestled with the angel by the river. (See Genesis 32:22–32.) After struggling all night with what he thinks is a man, Jacob realizes, "Hey, there's something different about this guy." So when the angel says, "Let me go," Jacob says, "No way. I'm not letting you go until you bless me." If this had been a proud statement, I believe the angel would have taken him out right there. Some theologians believe it was the Angel of the Lord, the preincarnate Christ, who was actually wrestling with Jacob. Jacob refuses to let go, so this angel hits him in his hip—hard.

I picture Jacob being dragged around by this angel, one leg trailing off to the side, and saying, "We might go for a wild ride. I'm dragging one leg now, but I am still not letting you go until you bless me. I am not letting you go until I know you are with me."

Finally, the angel asks, "What is your name?" When God asks you a question, it's not because He needs to know the answer. Jacob's name means "thief, usurper." The angel's question confronted Jacob with the truth of who he was without God: "I am nothing. I am a thief. God, You made this promise to me and I tried to bring it to pass on my own. But you know what? I get it now. I need You now. I am a thief and a usurper, a real jerk, without You."

Then the angel tells him, "Not anymore, Jacob. Something is different. I'm changing your name to Israel. I'm changing your name from 'thief' to 'prince.'"

What was the reason for the name change? The angel says, *"For you have struggled with God and with men, and have prevailed"* (Genesis 32:28). Let that sink in for a moment. "Jacob, I'm changing your name from 'thief' to 'prince' *because you wrestled with Me and you won.*"

God is longing for desperate people. It's not about who we are; it's about *who* we know. Those who know their God will do great exploits! (See Daniel 11:32.) It's time to cry out for God to break us out of every area where we have been settling and set us ablaze with His presence. If we do, I promise our lives will change and our understanding and expression of Christianity will never be boring again. We will be the most exciting, happy people in the world. Why? Because we will serve a very happy God.

Make no mistake—He is not "safe" and He is not tame. He's a consuming fire and His ministers are flames of fire. (See Psalm 104:4.) You are a flame of fire. So burn! Burn with His love! Light up the night and pierce this temporary present darkness with brilliant displays of His great love.

A PRAYER OF DESPERATION

Do you want more of the manifest presence, conviction, and power of the Holy Spirit? If your heart is stirred to cry out for the

Holy Spirit to baptize you with His fire and lead you into a radical lifestyle of following Him wherever He leads, I invite you to pray this prayer:

> Lord, when the disciples were on the road to Emmaus, You joined them and caused their hearts to burn as You spoke with them. Lord, I ask for that manifestation. Make my heart burn with fire and passion for Your presence again and again. Lord, I ask that I will be permeated, saturated, overwhelmed, and undone by Your Spirit. I want to be led by the cloud by day and the fire by night. I want to be like Ruth and say to You, "Where You go, I'll go. What You do, I'll do. Where You lodge, I'll lodge. I only want to be where You are." I give You permission to move everything that comes to separate me from You out of the way. Lord, I make a covenant with You that even if it costs everything, I will be led by the Spirit of the living God. It is not enough that I felt You move in me once. Move in me again. Fill me again. I am desperate for You. Thank You, Lord. Amen.

ABOUT THE AUTHOR

André T. Ashby was born in Kansas City, Missouri, where he came to know the Lord at an early age. He attended Oakwood Bible College in Huntsville, Alabama, majoring in religion, and later attended the University of Missouri Conservatory of Music, where he studied voice performance. André was also awarded a full scholarship to Grace Training Center at Metro Vineyard Fellowship in Kansas City, where he studied prophetic ministry. He is currently working on his music degree and minoring in biblical studies at William Jessup University.

André has traveled extensively across the United States and abroad, as a minister with Soul's Cry Ministries and the late Jill Austin of Master Potter Ministries. He has seen the Lord release the fire of God through the prophetic song and word, as well as spur people on to a deeper, more intimate relationship with Jesus. He is often used to release the Holy Spirit upon people in various settings. It has been said of André's unique and powerful ministry that he "carries the presence of God."

Welcome to Our House!

We Have a Special Gift for You

It is our privilege and pleasure to share in your love of Christian books. We are committed to bringing you authors and books that feed, challenge, and enrich your faith.

To show our appreciation, we invite you to sign up to receive a specially selected **Reader Appreciation Gift**, with our compliments. Just go to the Web address at the bottom of this page.

God bless you as you seek a deeper walk with Him!

WE HAVE A GIFT FOR YOU. VISIT:

whpub.me/nonfictionthx

WHITAKER
HOUSE